SECRET REGRETS™

What if you had a Second Chance?

Compiled by
Kevin Hansen

What People Are Saying About Secret Regrets*

"It's like an addiction. It's like I HAVE to peer into people's regrets. It's almost like therapy ... it helps me to appreciate it my own life more. It makes me realize that my regrets are little compared to others. It's always intriguing, interesting, sad, happy and has occasionally even saved someone's life!" – Shannon Couture

"I stumbled upon the Secret Regrets website by chance. It intrigued me enough that I posted my regret. Imagine my surprise when I returned to the site a few days later and saw my regret as the Regret of the Day. The comments people posted we encouraging. It was a good experience." – Donah Myers

"Secret Regrets let's people know they're not alone, and gives hope to those who think they are. Love the website! I'm on it everyday!" – Efia Sulter

FROM OUR @SECRETREGRETS TWITTER & FACEBOOK FANS:

"Yes ... I am currently addicted to Secret Regrets."

"So striking. So much of my own life in that of others."

"I seriously am in love with Secret Regrets right now. It's brilliant!"

"Secret Regrets will affect you in ways you never expected!"

"I posted my Secret Regret. That was good to get it off my chest."

"Secret Regrets is my escape."

"I just ate a whole bag of OH MY GOD when i checked out Secret Regrets!"

"Oh this is juicy!"

"Secret Regrets is legend – it's the only place some people can turn to for help"

Acknowledgements

I would like to extend a special "thank you" to my friends and family who have supported the development of the Secret Regrets project. Thank you to Gina Burkart for her encouragement, advice and help with proofing.

I would also like to thank the thousands of anonymous people who have revealed their innermost secret regrets at www.SecretRegrets.com. By reaching deep within yourself and allowing the world to share in your most personal thoughts, feelings and regretful experiences, your posts have helped countless people in ways you cannot begin to imagine. Thank you.

Kevin

If you like Secret Regrets, check out and contribute to our other projects:

www.LifeIsFunnyBlog.blogspot.com

www.MyDefiningMomentIs.blogspot.com

www.TheOnlyThingToFearIs.blogspot.com

www.TheWordsILiveBy.blogspot.com

www.MyPersonalCrossroads.blogspot.com

Dedicated to the love of my life. To my amazing wife, Connie.

Introduction

"I'm here."

Those two words that were posted on New Year's Day 2010 brought overwhelming relief to the followers of www.SecretRegrets.com. They were posted by a 16-year-old girl who two days prior had posted her intention to end her life on New Year's Eve. The reason? She felt that she didn't deserve to see 2010. Her post said that she regretted not having the courage to tell anyone about her intentions to overdose. She regretted how horrible it would be for the person who found her.

But then something amazing happened. The instant her original post went live, an unimaginable outpouring of support emerged for this young lady. Anonymous strangers began leaving comments, desperately trying to help her with her struggle. Crisis center websites and suicide hotline numbers were immediately posted. Many people bravely shared their own stories of overcoming their struggle with suicidal thoughts. And through it all, one common suggestion surfaced, "Just talk to someone."

Several people posted their personal e-mail addresses in hopes of communicating directly with the poster. Others even posted their phone numbers, offering to be there – to just talk, listen or whatever.

For nearly 48 hours, the Secret Regrets community waited to hear something – anything at all – to confirm she had read the supportive comments left by these compassionate strangers. Comments letting her know she was not alone. Letting her know she was loved, and how she deserved to not only see 2010, but to see what her entire life had in store for her.

And then, at 1:53 PM on New Year's Day, the message we had all been waiting for finally arrived. It started with,

"I'm here."

Here's what followed:

"Thank you guys for all your comments, they really made me think. They made me feel strong enough to let my friend help me. She talked to her mum who talked to mine. I was taken to the doctor, and have another appointment soon.

I AM GETTING HELP.

I seriously wish I could thank every one of you personally. You guys now mean so much.

Happy New Year!"

She took a brave step in revealing her deepest, darkest, secret regret. And the Secret Regrets community responded with loving, non-judgmental, and sympathetic open arms. Arms that reached out from all over the world to wrap themselves around a hurting, young soul, who needed someone to listen, understand, and to be there for her.

"I'm here," were the words she selected to let everyone know she was OK. And ironically, they were also the words chosen by complete strangers to let her know that someone – many people in fact – were in reality, there for her.

Preface

Over the past decade, the World Wide Web has made a quantum leap in its ability to connect people. Facebook allows long lost friends to reconnect. LinkedIn allows professionals to connect and network with their peers. Sites like Match and eHarmony connect singles searching for their perfect soul mates.

Along the way, other types of sites and blogs started popping up, allowing people to connect with each other anonymously. A few of the more popular sites centered around people's confessions and secrets. I was very intrigued by this phenomenon, and in 2007 decided to start a blog that went one step farther. Instead of providing an outlet for people to simply reveal secrets, I wanted to create a forum that allowed people to acknowledge and admit their regrets. And not just any regret – but the BIGGEST regret of their lives. The ONE thing they would do differently if they had a second chance.

The goal of this project?

To help people see how powerful "looking back" can be as the first step in "moving forward."

After the Secret Regrets blog went live, something happened over the next couple of months that I wasn't expecting. Something that showed me the tremendous impact this site had. People began leaving amazing comments on many of the Secret Regrets posted on the site. Some of the comments totally blew me away. I was astounded by the words of encouragement, support, sympathy, empathy and love that were left by complete strangers. And often, the anonymous person who posted the original regret would come back and leave comments on what they did after they read the reader comments. Many posters thanked those who shared their insights – expressing how their comments helped them see their regrets in a different light.

Every day, more and more people began visiting and reading the blog, and more and more people began posting their own Secret Regrets. What developed proved a universal truth – that no matter what you are facing in your life, you are not alone.

Someone out there can relate to what you are going through – and may have even made it through a similar situation. These people are not doctors, therapists or other clinically trained professionals. Instead they are wives, husbands, girlfriends, boyfriends, mothers, fathers, brothers, sisters, friends, bosses, co-workers, lovers and exes – real people with real life experiences and real life perspectives. They are sympathetic to what you are going through. And they want to help.

It didn't take long to realize there was a tremendous opportunity to use this project to help others. Many supporters of the Secret Regrets site have requested that I put together a book featuring some of the most impactful regrets submitted. So I did, and you're holding that book in your hands. My hope is that if you're tormented by something you regret, that one or more of the regrets in the book help you realize there are others dealing with the same kinds of tough life experiences. My wish is that inside these pages, you'll find strength, encouragement and hope. No matter what you are struggling with, remember, you have the caring support of the entire Secret Regrets community ready to help you through.

Peace,

Kevin

Please Note: Although the Secret Regrets project provides useful insight, it is in no way a substitute for professional help and advice. It is simply thoughts, opinions and stories from real, everyday people. If you are facing serious challenges that you don't know how to deal with, please seek out additional help. And don't stop until you get it. Talk to a teacher, someone at church, a trusted relative or friend and ask them to help you find the professional help you need. Call a crisis line or center.

You can also visit **www.ReachOut.com**. It's a great site for teens and young adults (and even not-so-young adults) where you can find out how others got through a tough time – or learn how you can help people you know who are going through a tough time. The site has lots of useful information and resources, like the "Get Help" section that lists many hotlines and support centers that you can call for help.

Another great source for hotlines and helplines can also be found at:
www.healthyplace.com/other-info/resources/mental-health-hotline-numbers-and-referral-resources/menu-id-200/

SECRET REGRETS

What if you had a Second Chance?

SECRET REGRET: I regret all the praying that I've done to keep you on this earth, Mom. I know how much pain you're in and how badly you want it all to stop. I know that you'd be better off in Heaven with God. I know.

I regret my selfishness of wanting to keep you.

I still don't want God to take you, but would it be best?

I need you Mom.

Just stay for a little while longer.

Please, for me.

COMMENTS:

>> I could have written this regret. My mother just passed a few months ago and I feel guilty everyday that when she stopped breathing, I so desperately wanted to breathe for her to keep her here with me. I know that the day she died was the happiest day of her life; she is no longer suffering as she was here with us. Take comfort in that fact. There is nothing I can say to take away the pain, but try to keep the good times forefront in your mind. Your mother will always be with you, even if you can't see her.

>> Don't feel guilty for wanting your mother to continue living. Very few people on this planet would feel any different in your situation.

>> I regret this same thing still, seven years after I finally said "I let go mom, I'll see you when I get there too." To this day I wish that I hadn't been the one holding on, saying, "No, you won't die, you have to live."

>> Your mother would have wanted to stay for you, regardless of the pain. I have 2 kids, and if it's in my power I will stay for them until they're ready to let me go. Your mama knew you loved her and she knew you wanted her with you – I can't imagine a better thing for a mother to know as she was passing.

www.SecretRegrets.com

SECRET REGRET: I regret friending you on Facebook. Now I see your life without me every time you post a status update. Technology means never having to say goodbye forever. Female, 20

COMMENTS:

>> Oh, man. I can so relate to this regret ... Ugh.

>> I have the same problem. I deleted my ex off Facebook but I often use friends' accounts to see how happy he is without me. I still love him. 2 years later.

>> I know how you feel. I follow my ex's every move on Twitter and I know all about the lives of him and his friends. I know that it's not healthy and I should stop following him, but I just can't. I need to remain connected to him in some way. I'm not ready to cut him out of my life yet, as much as I want to be.

>> More than 25 people agreed that the poster should definitely delete, block or unfriend him – and just move on.

SECRET REGRET: You were a baby, I was 18, my boyfriend was violent. I regret being too scared to stand up for you and me, instead they took you away. That was 20 years ago. I think about you every day. I regret my other children will never know you, their sister ...

I regret that you will never know that although I had lost you to another family, you were the one that gave me the courage to leave in the end! I regret the years that followed with your brothers and sister and how scared I was to love them in case I messed it up! I regret the pain this has caused so many people, but most of all I regret the pain it has caused you.

When I found you on the internet, I could not believe the pain you were causing yourself and the harm you were doing to your soul. I regret not telling you that your online friend was me ... I'm sorry, I always will be sorry ... but what can I do now!!!????

It's too late ...

COMMENTS:

>> Tell! Please! Just tell! It might change your, and your child's life!

>> As a fellow mother, my heart breaks for you. You're obviously in so much pain. Tell her who you are. She may not realize it, but she needs to know. She will love you. And then both of you, please go see a therapist. Take care of yourselves!

SECRET REGRET: There is a man that always follows me but he doesn't exist. I can feel his eyes on my back and his hands around my neck. I don't know what he looks like because he is only a shadow.

I regret not telling anyone and forcing myself to live like this.

I don't know if he was real at one point or will be real in the future. But I have this overwhelming feeling that he has hurt me already.

I think this is a dark part of my childhood coming back at me. I regret being too scared to ask someone for answers.

19/f

COMMENTS:

>> I know this feeling very well. Counseling helps and so does time. Eventually you will either face it head on, or acknowledging its presence will help the "hidden memories" fade. I've got 8 years on you. At 19, I hadn't even seen the shadows, just felt them all around. You have time.

SECRET REGRET: I regret the fact that we're $50,000 in debt (outside of mortgage and cars) and that you have no idea. You hate your job so much, and if we didn't have this debt, I could support you in walking away.

SECRET REGRET: I was there when the doctor told you about the cancer. I held your hand as you cried and screamed, "I don't want to die." We shared more after that than ever. I loved the time we spent. I'll never regret that ...

But I do regret running when it got bad. You didn't know me. And it hurt. I regret practically living with my girlfriend whom you didn't approve of. We're apart now.

I regret the day hospice came the most. Because I left the house and didn't come back that night ...

And you didn't live to see me the next day.

I regret abandoning you in your final days.

I miss you and love you Mom.

24 M

COMMENTS:

>> Don't let this eat at you anymore. You have to be a parent to know that she would never blame you. She loves you, even now, and forever. She has gone home, and the two of you will be together one day. Till then know she is with you every minute.

>> I had cancer. I have it again. It makes people react differently. It scares the hell out of us, and what scares the hell out of us even more is when we think of what it might do to our kids, our family. Don't think for a moment that your mom doesn't understand. We do! And I for one, wished my kids (17 and 13 the first round), never had to hear me throw up, or pace the floor from the radiation shakes. I wished time and time again that they could be somewhere else. Or that I could be. Your mom knows you love her to this day. Regrets are for the dying ... honor her by being one of the living. Make a difference to another person with cancer. Walk, run, fundraise, read to a patient, donate marrow, blood. That's what makes us moms proud. So take it from this survivor and fighter ... she loves you, show her the love back.

SECRET REGRET: I regret saying I didn't like the ring and I didn't like the way you proposed. It was shallow and stupid of me. I know you did the best you could for me and I was still ungrateful and I've always felt horrible for it. Because now, I wish for nothing more than you to put a ring on my finger and call me your fiancé again.

COMMENTS:

>> 25 years ago I dropped out of college to work and save and be able to go back, and spent more than I should have on a ring. I proposed in a way I thought you would like, but the look of disappointment on your face when you saw the ring was devastating. It was the best I could do, and really more than I could afford. I went back to school, met someone who understood how poor I was. 23 years later she still wears the $80 ring I proposed with great pride. I'm really glad you reacted like you did, it exposed the real you and prompted me to leave while it only cost me a ring. Thanks!

SECRET REGRET: I wish that I would have listened to your cries for help and that I would have helped you. I am so sorry that we were in a fight and I honestly thought that midterms were more important than talking to you. I am so sorry that I let you kill yourself and I was the only person that you reached out to. It has been 7 years and this guilt is killing me very slowly every day that I live. I wish I could join you so I wouldn't have to live like this anymore, but I can't because I know how much suicide destroys people's lives. Since you have left, every relationship I have is f'd up. I miss you so much. I am so sorry that I couldn't help you, that I was too self-centered. I love you Dad.

F/27

COMMENTS:

>> A 20 year old is not supposed to be responsible for being her father's therapist. I had to learn that lesson with my own father. Depression is a form of mental illness, and you were not equipped or trained to fix it. It was much bigger than you. This is not your fault. Get professional help with this, forgive yourself. I pray that you find peace.

---

www.SecretRegrets.com

SECRET REGRET: No words can express how much regret I feel for typing out last week on this site about how madly in love I am with the other guy ... because today my boyfriend did something for me that only a man soul-heartedly in love with his girlfriend would do.

SECRET REGRET: I regret tracking you down on the internet just over a year ago.

I regret idly typing your name into a search engine one day and coming up with an article from the local press about your recent wedding.

I regret tracing the website of your photographer and trawling through the dozens of photographs of your wedding with my heart pounding and my mouth run dry, in shock. In those photos, you look so very happy. Your hair is graying now, your waistline a little thicker but your smile takes my breath away, still. Your bride is beautiful and you are looking into her eyes. I've seen that look so many times before, it's the look you gave me when it was me that you loved. I dream about you still, less often than I did. I wake up feeling so empty and when I tell my husband I had a bad dream, I don't mention that you were in it, still loving me.

I regret that I was not the one for you. I regret that you were unable to keep on loving me.

I regret ever having been so loved by and in love with you. How could anything ever compare to that?

I regret that I have a loving husband, happy, healthy children, good friends and a comfortable life and it will never be enough.

I regret knowing that I would give up everything I have (and I have so much) to be with you again and for the rest of my life.

I regret that I will only ever be in your arms again in my dreams.

I regret that it has been 18 long years since you left me and that the pain has never gone away.

COMMENTS:

>> You need to let it go or else you will ruin the life you have now.

>> He was never really mine, either.

>> We are all guilty of romanticizing past relationships and some of us just get stuck in this perpetual "what if" state of mind. It's so dangerous to do this. You risk not only ruining your own life (which you admit is good and full), but that of your husband and your children as well. It's so easy to imagine that your life with someone else would have been so much more exciting, romantic, fulfilling, etc. because your relationship with that person never made it beyond the "warm and fuzzy" honeymoon years. The fact of the matter is, the two of you broke up for a reason. And there is no happily ever after. No long-term relationship is without its arguments and resentments and doubts. No matter who you're in that relationship with. If your relationship with this man had worked out, chances are you'd be having similar thoughts about someone else. And that doesn't make you a bad person, as I said, we're all guilty of this to some degree. Just don't ruin the happiness that's right in front of you for something that never existed.

SECRET REGRET: I regret complaining about us walking too slowly. I regret complaining about you leaning on me for balance. It was so much harder for you, being handicapped. I was just a kid.

I'm sorry, Mom.

Now more than anything I want to be your crutch.

COMMENTS:

>> You were just a kid ... don't beat yourself up. It's not easy being able-bodied and understanding someone's disability. Just let your mom know you love her and that you're there for her no matter what. My husband is now disabled and it's been a tough adjustment for both of us, and I have to keep reminding myself that he's the same person on the inside, just a little different on the outside now.

SECRET REGRET: I regret that I let him hurt me so bad, that I can't trust you. I don't want you to move on, I want you to wait for me to get over him. I hate that I fell for the asshole and now I can't commit myself to the sweetheart.

F/17

COMMENTS:

>> Speaking as the "sweetheart" in this situation ... pick either to work at this relationship, and show him every day that it means the world to you that he's being patient, or let him go. I spent most of a year with someone who was hung up on an ex. Every day I spent with him was an agony of not knowing if he even wanted me to hold on, and now I'm the one too hung up on an ex to move on. Don't jerk around a good guy ... make a decision about what you want and act on it. Now.
>> Sorry that you got hurt. You have to heal but you cannot expect for someone to wait for you. Concentrate on you and when you are ready for a relationship, you will find someone. All the best. I have been there too and it took me 2 years and I'm still a work in progress.

SECRET REGRET: I regret that you are the kind of person who is satisfied with the life we have now. I'm not satisfied. I still love you and I don't want to break up our family but living like this every day while we take each other for granted is so sad. I try to start interesting conversations and plan things for us to do together without the kids and initiate sex and it doesn't seem like you even notice my effort. Seems like you are going through the motions.

The worst part of this is that there is a man who has been loving me and wanting me for over 25 years. He adores me now. He loves me now and wants me now. Every time we talk he lets me know how important I am to him. He tells me he loves me many times a day. He makes me feel so much more loved than you do and I have not seen him in over 10 years. I wonder if you would say you loved me ever again if I stopped saying it first? I cannot break up my family. I regret that you are the kind of person who could live like this happily forever. It's killing me. I regret that you will never get dissatisfied enough to leave me.

F/41

COMMENTS:

>> You sound like you really want things to work out but your husband doesn't get it or ignores the efforts. When you do all you can possibly do, then it is time to let go. To let go is not to regret the past but to grow and live for the future. All the best.

>> If you want to make it work with your husband, then let go of the other guy … how can you really work on your marriage if you are still thinking about someone else? Maybe your husband sees that in you but doesn't know how to approach you about it.

SECRET REGRET: The one thing I regret the most was having to leave you behind. You didn't know what was going on, only that we had left. I will never forget the look on your face as we drove away, as you stood there watching us. Somehow, in that instant, I knew that you knew that we would not be back. I'm so sorry that no one cared for you after we left. I know that eventually someone watched over you, but it still broke my heart to hear that you were not eating. I am so sorry that you had to watch as your children were taken from you, against your will, and that you never saw them again. I cannot imagine the pain you felt. I regret that you did not have a better family, one that could take care of you to the end. I regret that you had to die alone without your children nearby.

You were the best dog that I will ever have, and I miss you terribly. Wherever you are, I hope you can see this, and know that I wish things could have been different. I wish I could go back in time to have brought you with me. I hope that you know that I loved and still do love you. I regret that my parents had such a nasty divorce, and that you had to bear the consequences as well. It wasn't fair to you. Wherever you are now, know that I will always regret losing my best friend.

COMMENTS:

>> My puppy is sitting on my bed with me, and by the end of reading your story I was bawling. He knew it wasn't your fault that you had to go; I hope that eventually you can find some peace of mind. Our animals are so dependent on us for love and acceptance, I think grown ups can forget that sometimes.

>> Sooo sad … this REALLY makes me miss my cat. I had to leave her behind too.

>> It was really only after realizing it was about a dog that tears started to well up. Last year I had

to put down the dog I had for 16 years. It was one of the hardest things I ever had to do. I still cry whenever I think about him. I believe animals go to heaven, you'll see him again someday.

>> This one made me cry at work (and I'm a guy). It sounds to me like you and your dog were equal casualties of your parents' divorce. I am so sorry for you and your dog. I pray that you find comfort from this.

SECRET REGRET: I regret wishing you were dead and feeling disappointed when you came home alive.

COMMENTS:

>> This could be someone I know. And I hate you with everything I have for you wishing I died.

>> I hope that things get better for you, whatever your situation.

SECRET REGRET: I regret putting those videos on YouTube and Facebook. I regret singing in them. Now, as a freshman in high school, I am ridiculed daily for doing so. I definitely regret letting their snide comments get to me and crying over them. I shouldn't care. But I do. A lot. And I regret that.

COMMENTS:

>> I think it's impressive that you made videos, sang in them and posted them to the internet. That takes guts, it takes passion ... don't give that up because of rotten people. When you're older, these jerks won't matter. Live your life the way that makes you happy. You matter, they don't.

>> Anna, just know I used to make comments about your videos and sometimes still do (old habits die hard). But now that I know you, I think you are braver than everyone else at school for putting yourself out there. Even braver than me.

SECRET REGRET: I regret all the times I've held back feelings even when everyone knows something's wrong. The truth really does set you free ...

COMMENTS:

>> This secret was really touching for me. I know exactly what you are going through, for I do the exact same thing. I truly hope that you will open up to someone before anything goes too far. People are there to listen, help you, and support you, no matter how difficult life may get. I know it's hard to express your emotions when you've been hiding them for your entire life but trust me, it will all be worth it once you let it out.

SECRET REGRET: I regret the fact that my mother aborted the other child and not me, and that every day I let her remind me of how big a mistake that was on her part.

COMMENTS:

>> My mom had two abortions before she had me, and I only believe she kept me in hopes of keeping my biological father. Hardly a day goes by that I wish I wasn't the first or second abortion.

>> I'm so sorry that your mother would even dream of saying something like that to you. Don't let her words bring you down or get in the way of the life that you've been given.

SECRET REGRET: If I had a second chance, I would have had the guts to break up with my girlfriend (now ex) and kiss you. Those 8 weeks were the most amazing time I've ever had. I thought I was in love with her, and yet when I met you it showed me a whole different perspective on life. You were, and are, the only one who I can fully be myself around. I fully opened my heart to you, and you returned the favor, and yet I still backed away, I still didn't have the balls to just go and kiss you. I think about you every day, and it's been 2 years. It haunts me to know that you now have moved on and won't ever feel the same way about me (and it's my fault we aren't together), even though when I hear your name, no matter the context, my heart skips a beat. It sucks to live off a street that is your name, it sucks that so many things remind me of that summer. All I wanted to do was be with you, and yet I was too scared to cheat on my girlfriend (or just break up with her), only thinking of the consequences and not the fact the pros outweighed the cons by an immeasurable amount. My goal in life is to find a girl like you, and I haven't found anyone who comes close. Every part of you was amazing, the personality, the way you move, your laugh, your eyes. The worst is when I have dreams about you, and wake up and realize they aren't real ... and it brings me to tears. My view is that I'm being selfish, so I don't confront you about it. All I want for you is to be happy, and from what I can tell you are. Maybe one day it'll all come out into the open. I just hope it doesn't ruin our friendship.

Male 18

COMMENTS:

>> You should definitely tell her how you feel. Maybe you should show this to her so she can read it for herself and understand why you didn't take the leap way back when.

>> GO AFTER HER!!!

>> If I were her I would want you to tell me.

SECRET REGRET: My biggest regret was following him on the rectory. I allowed him to steal my youth and my beliefs all in one action. I regret never telling anyone or stopping him. I regret that my lack of action means others probably also suffered.

I regret every belief I lost due to this act.

42 / male

SECRET REGRET: I regret that every time we get a phone call to say you've drunk yourself into the hospital again I hope that this time you won't make it out. Partly so that you'll stop hurting everyone around you, and partly because it seems like a dead brother would be a good story to tell.

22/F

COMMENTS:

>> I share the same regret, except it is my husband ...

>> I have a dead brother. Trust me, it is not a good story.

>> I have the same brother and I completely understand how you feel. People who haven't been thru this can't possibly begin to understand. They think it is cruel and hateful. And it is not a matter of not helping him; God knows we have all tried. It is a matter of him not helping himself. And now it it's too late for him to change, he is just trying to kill himself slowly. The pain this causes is unbearable. I would give anything for it to be different but it is not, and it is not something anyone else can control but him.

SECRET REGRET: If I could change one thing, I would have stood up to my parents when I was younger. I never stood up for my beliefs with them and now I don't know how to stand up to anyone. I try to make my voice heard with them now. But it normally ends up with a debate. I still can't find the courage to tell my mom that I feel like she's made me who I am today. And it's not someone I'm proud of. I'm scared of the world, I won't stand up for myself, and I find it oh-so-hard to say, "no" to anything I don't really want to do. I don't know if it's unfair that I blame her for everything. And I feel bad saying it. I feel bad for saying or doing anything "mean" ... or that could be construed as mean. I believe that if I had seen through my mother's "I'm a victim" way of life and stood up to it, I would be a completely different person. Not the lost, confused little girl that I've become.

Female, 24

COMMENTS:

>> I know what you're going through! I feel your pain and it took me many years and many friends to help pull me out of it. It's tough to think about, but you don't need her ... she needs you more, that's why she acts that way. Try telling her that you just want her to be a friend like a mother should instead of the controlling person she is. If it doesn't work, move on from her. She'll eventually realize what she's done. I'll say a prayer for you that you can find that.

---

www.SecretRegrets.com

SECRET REGRET: My biggest regret is that I ever started cheating on my husband. Every time I do it, I say it's the last time, but it never is. I don't know how to stop and I feel so guilty about it. The only thing I am getting out of it is the realization that I have the perfect man and I don't deserve him one bit.

SECRET REGRET: If I could go back, I would have said no. Your praise isn't worth the tears. M/15

SECRET REGRET: I regret sending nude pics to my at-the-time boyfriend. I didn't want to, he made me feel bad about not doing it, so I did. We got into a big fight and the truth about him came out. He sent them around our school, more than once. A year later, they ended up online where not only did my whole school see them, but a bunch of other schools in the area did, too. I was 14 when the pictures were taken. 15 when they were exposed to the internet.

COMMENTS:

>> I'm sorry that someone took such horrible advantage of you. If your ex boyfriend posted those pictures online – or even just distributed them around, he can be charged with child porn, as you were a minor when those pictures were taken. Something to think about (charging him). It will surely make him and any of the other assholes that passed these pictures around think twice about what they're doing. Also, it would a great way to get him back for what he did to you. You didn't deserve that, but he deserves to pay.

>> This happened to my little sister and every day I regret not being able to make it better. I bumped into one of the guys that did it to her a while back and threatened him with all my being, not the right thing to do I'm sure but I remember the smile on her face. Don't be afraid to report this, it will mean you are taking a stand for yourself and anyone else it may happen to. No one will think badly of you for it. Those who know of the situation will learn that you respect yourself and in turn they should too AND you will get to see whoever distributed these pictures squirm like the worms they are when faced with the consequences.

>> I'm sorry this happened to you but if you try to charge him it is possible that you can be charged as well in this case since you did send the pictures to him. Teenagers have short memories when it comes to things like this – no one in your school will remember it in a year. Just try to let it go.

SECRET REGRET: To my father: I regret that I never told you I loved you until you were dying. I regret thinking I had a horrible childhood. You worked so hard to take care of my brothers and me. I regret hating you for keeping such a close eye on me in my teenage years.

You were the only one who believed in me and the only person who loved me enough to push me to do better. You made me into the person I am today. I love you so much and I wish I could take back every mean thing I ever said to you.

I regret the day I had to take you off life support and realize all this.

F/23

COMMENTS:

>> I'm so sorry you've had to go though this and I hope that one day you'll truly know in your heart that your father loved you dearly.

>> I don't usually believe in "signs" or whatever, but recently my dad and I have been clashing. By recently, I mean throughout my childhood up to this point. Just last night, he told me he loved me and I said "ok." I hope to never be in the position you have been in and are currently in, but thank you for sharing this so hopefully I can start being a better daughter now, before it gets to a life and death situation. I'm praying for you.

>> I understand. I didn't know how bad my relationship with my father had gotten until he was gone. I wish he were here so I could tell him how much I love him and how much he shaped my life. He made me who I am today; He made me a better mom.

SECRET REGRET: I regret not being more of a man when I was 16.

If I'd been stronger for her when she told me she was pregnant, then maybe she wouldn't have taken the life of herself and our unborn child.

Exactly ten years later, and I've sabotaged every relationship I've had since. I regret that I've hurt so many beautiful, sensitive women by being unable to make real the emotions I feign.

I WANT the emotions, but I can't have a future with anyone, because I can't help but see her face and that of our daughter that never was. Lily would have been so pretty.

COMMENTS:

>> I think you've punished yourself enough. We all do things we regret when we are younger; we do not know the weight of our actions and our words on others. You know now that you made a mistake, and you feel the weight and guilt of it. I think if you were to replay those moments and days now, you would do things differently. And while you cannot do that, that's what counts. Please lift your chin and live for yourself now. It's the least you can do for her, isn't it? Be at peace with yourself, because you'll only make things harder for yourself. You weren't a man then, but you're a man now, and be the man now that you wish you could be. Be strong and overcome your sadness and guilt.

>> I've been through a suicidal depression, and I can honestly say that in that place, your mind is so disturbed that you honestly think that killing yourself is doing the people you love a favor. That you'll make things better for them by not being there. It's not your fault, and she wouldn't want this for you.

>> You made mistakes. You have paid long enough. You are not responsible for her actions. Even if you contributed to feelings, etc. she CHOSE to end her life. You did not do that for her. The hardest, most horrible things in our pasts can make us stronger. You have the ability to be a great MAN and FATHER! But you would be wise to work through these things with a professional so that you will believe that is true. God bless you!

>> (Update from the original poster): To all of you who have posted, thank you. I told my current partner two days ago. She held me and I cried for the first time in 8 years. She understands now why I've been so distant and shut off, and together she's helping me get the help I need.

SECRET REGRET: If I had a second chance to do one thing differently in my life, I wouldn't have let you control me. I wouldn't have let you ruin my childhood and all the learning experiences I could have had. I'm now stuck in a world where I can't do anything for myself. I don't know how. And you blame me for not doing more with my life, when you're the one who made me this way.

Female 20

SECRET REGRET: I would treat her better than I did back then. I'm still completely in love with her and know now that I could treat her like a princess. Because that's what she is to me. And no one will treat you better than I can Kait. That's a promise.

22/f

COMMENTS:

>> I wish that "Kait" were "Sarah."

>> I wish that "Kait" were Rachel. I wish Kylee regretted what she did to me.

SECRET REGRET: I regret ever allowing you into my life. How could I have known then? I was a 6th grader, not yet twelve years old. When we first met, you were the gym teacher in the adjacent Jr. High. Our chance encounters at that time were random, but you made a point to be friendly to me. You groomed me for the next three years, helped me with my sports, made me laugh, laughed with me, told me jokes and stories, taught me some Yiddish, you even helped me when I realized that the boy I had a crush on was already a drunk. You guided me through some of the roughest times of my early teen years.

When you were about to lose me, the summer before I left for high school, you made your move. I was 15. You were 30. You took from me the innocence of my youth, not to mention my virginity. Because I was under a Quaalude induced high, I do not remember losing it. Again and again that summer I gave myself to you. You introduced me to drugs, alcohol and sex.

www.SecretRegrets.com

There is SO much more that I could have told:
The accident,
hospital,
court,
California.

You never left me alone.
We spanned a more than a decade.

I did not fully understand the impact of the relationship between you and I until too late.

I f'd up many years of my life.
I take responsibility and know that my actions stem from your actions.

I began talking to my beautiful daughter, now almost 13, at 3 and 4 years of age about being aware of teachers, of how no one can make you feel special, or what it is like to lose a part of childhood, and of trust.

I would like the world to know:
YOU ARE SCUM!
and
I HATE YOU!

COMMENTS:

>> My heart goes out to you. This man hurt you but you now have a child that is looking up to you for everything. Please get help and heal yourself so that you can take care of your child. I wish you well and will pray for you

>> Try to release the hatred and forgive. What this man did will never be okay, but you are only hurting yourself and your child by holding on to such a painful past.

SECRET REGRET: My wonderful sweet babies, I regret that I was such a self-centered mother. I regret that I didn't take more time with each of you and show you better what amazing and capable little people you were. I regret that I didn't teach you better ways

nore structure into your little lives. I regret that I
ork with you. I regret that I didn't force you, my
of your diabetes. I regret that I didn't instruct you
w to eat properly and how to fix dinner and keep a
over these things I didn't do. I taste the bitterness
ults but suffer so because I didn't teach you some
nore feeling this heavy and unbearable guilt.

ther, I can say that I struggle daily with being disorganized and
the way my mom raised me made me who I am and I know
eep things afloat and keeping us fed. I appreciate all that she did
didn't do. I carry it with me in hopes that I do things differently
d, so just be proud that you did the best you could at the time.

SECRET REGRET: If I had a second chance, I would have never let those words past my lips. I would NEVER have said, "I hate you!"

And if I couldn't change it, if those words flew out of anger anyway, I would have chased after you. Begged you to forgive me. Taken those words back before you were taken from me. You were so young when you died. I was young, too. But that doesn't excuse those three words. It doesn't make up for letting you leave, still upset.

If I could change it, maybe I could have lived my life the way you hoped I would. Maybe I would be a better person. Maybe I would have never become an addict. Maybe you would have died that night anyway. But maybe, just maybe, if I hadn't let those words be the last thing I said to you, I could learn to love myself even without you in my life.

I miss you so much. And I'm so sorry.

F/20

SECRET REGRET: I regret that during this Christmas season, I have not been able to turn to God to help my family get through some tough times. I try to handle this all myself, and carry the burden single-handedly. I know He's there to help, but I'm either too proud to ask – or too scared of how He'll answer.

COMMENTS:

>> Keep in mind that God has His own agenda, but speaking from personal experience and cases of extreme personal hardship (my mom dying when I was 17 for instance), I do know that God has a plan with everything He does. You might not understand certain situations or circumstances now, but give it time, and trust in Him.

SECRET REGRET: If I had a second chance to do ONE thing differently in my life, I would've manned up and had the balls to ask you on a date. I wouldn't have taken the easy path and just gotten to be friends, and gotten to the point where we're close enough it'd be too weird to ask. I wouldn't have been afraid that you didn't like me that way, or that it would ruin a friendship we already had. I wouldn't have been afraid of what my friends would have said about you – screw them. I wouldn't have asked your friend to homecoming instead of you. I would've changed my mind and asked you instead when I realized I made a mistake, and when there was still time to.

The thing is, I think I still have a chance. But I AM too afraid still. I don't really know why else I keep making you think I only want to be friends.

Male, 17

COMMENTS:

>> Tell her. She's probably already fallen for you too. If not, your friendship is probably strong enough to withstand it. I told my best friend once and he wasn't interested and our friendship didn't change a bit. And now I'm so thankful for our friendship – taught me to trust guys again and still provides advice and I'm so glad we never dated. I'm engaged to another man.

>> From a girl's perspective, ask her out!!! I'm in the same position right now except as the girl and it absolutely kills me that I'm so close with this one guy and I know he likes me, but he's too nervous about change to ask me out. Just do it!!!

>> Ask her! That kind of bravery in guys is rare and valuable. If she truly cares about you as a friend, then she will respect you in your vulnerability no matter what. Chances are, she's been wondering for years why the heck you haven't made a move and whether you like her.

SECRET REGRET: I need to tell him how much I like him, how his smile makes me forget what I'm thinking about. But I can't, because sometimes not knowing is better than being rejected. I regret not taking the chances that may result in happiness because I'm too scared.

COMMENTS:

>> I was in the same position. We were friends for 5 years. It would've been "weird" to ever "be together." But I took that chance, and little did I know that he was feeling the exact same as me. And it turned out to be the most amazing relationship I've ever had … and he's the most amazing guy … because we were friends before, our love was rooted in friendship, so it was strong. **Please take the chance. Don't keep living in pain and let someone else win him over.** Don't miss your chance.

SECRET REGRET: I regret losing my virginity in a car in an empty parking lot. Happy Birthday Will. F/19

COMMENTS:

>> Now that you know how that experience made you feel, don't ever settle again … you're too good for that … hugs to you … =)

>> Thank you for posting this. It makes me feel like I'm not the only who settled when I deserve so much more. I regret losing my virginity in a car in an empty parking lot … happy high school graduation Trev.

>> I lost mine in a car on the side of the road. Happy Birthday Tom.

SECRET REGRET: I regret that I confessed to something I didn't do to protect you. I know now that you wouldn't have done the same thing for me. So much for so called friends.

Female 21

SECRET REGRET: If I had a second chance to do ONE thing differently in my life, I would not have put my job before my family because it gave my husband a reason to have an affair and I totally understand it now. Not that it makes it right, I just understand that he wasn't the only person to blame. F/38

COMMENTS:

>> Do not blame yourself for your husband's poor choices. An affair is never the answer, remedy, or solution ... for ANYTHING. You were neglectful, he was unfaithful. There is no justified correlation or causation there.

>> I kind of disagree with the first poster. If you were neglected in a marriage, you'd probably feel the urge to cheat too. Not saying it's right, but it's not entirely the husband's fault. Even if it was his choice, it's a human thing to do when you feel neglected. Anyway, I hope you work things out for the best.

>> I think that if you are feeling neglected the first human feeling should be to talk to your spouse about it before cheating. Cheating is a poor decision made by the cheater. In this case, it is not her fault that her husband cheated. If he really loved her, and wanted things to work out, he wouldn't have cheated. He would have told her "Hey, we need to do something about this, or I'm going to have to consider alternatives." And those alternatives could have been therapy, separation, or divorce. But just cheating before trying to work things out is a cop out.

>> (Update from the original poster): This was actually my regret I wrote. I was shocked to visit the website today and see it was posted. For an update, while I will never condone what happened I just don't put all the blame on him. It's been 4 years now, almost to the day and our marriage is better than it's ever been. There is a lot of open communication about everything from the kids to the money. There is also respect now that we didn't have before. Thanks everyone for posting.

SECRET REGRET: I regret applying for the university where I'm studying right now, when I could have done much better. I regret saying to my boyfriend that I wanted him to come with me when I left the country, because he took it seriously, and I was just small talking.

SECRET REGRET: If I could change one thing I would have appreciated my mom when she still wanted to be a mom. Now, after her affair and divorce, I would give anything for a mom.

SECRET REGRET: I regret being the girl you met after your girlfriend passed away, because that's all I ever was and will be. I regret that I ever thought I was enough to make you smile again, and that I thought I could ever be more to you than a temporary fix. I regret every day that I fell for you when you never had any intention of falling for me.

SECRET REGRET: I should have left him the first time he hit me. Those three months are my biggest regret. My family still talks about "that nice boy" and asks why I won't speak to him. I'm too ashamed to tell them.

COMMENTS:

>> You have nothing to be ashamed of. Just be glad you're out of it now and able to find someone that deserves you.

>> Regret that you didn't leave the first time he hit you. But NEVER regret that you left. Be so PROUD of yourself and especially be so PROUD that you left after a SHORT period. Some women stay their WHOLE LIVES. I left after 4 years and having a child. My child saved me. I couldn't let her grow up like that. And I am PROUD of myself. And I am PROUD of you.

---

www.SecretRegrets.com

SECRET REGRET: I regret making fun of you in sixth grade Maggie. I regret that I stayed up with a friend and thought of fat jokes that we could say to you the next day. I can't believe what a horrible little kid I was. I still think about it 14 years later. I wish for the day when I can tell you how sorry I am. What's more, I wish that if that day were to come, you would tell me to get over myself because it didn't affect you at all.

COMMENTS:

>> I was the one being ridiculed and I am also one of the girls that people thought it never bothered b/c I was so confident and outgoing. Trust me. I cried myself to sleep, hated looking in mirrors, shopping with anyone, being stared at in public and looked at as nothing more than one of the guys to crush. I am 21 now, things are different, but I'm still made fun of by ignorant men in bars. Go to this person, even if it's a letter or message on Facebook. An apology won't change the past, but it might at least make the future more bearable. I don't like that you were a person who made fat jokes, but it helps that you are wise enough now to realize it was wrong. People are people and deserve to be treated as such regardless of size. I hope you find peace.

>> Guilt is hard to live with. And so is torment.

SECRET REGRET: I don't know what I regret more in my life at this second – falling in love with you, waiting so long to tell you, or sending you that, "I need to ask you something," text message because I was too terrified to ask you in person.

You still haven't replied to that message, and it's been about eight hours. I don't know if you're just being lazy and not checking your phone (which you do a lot) or aren't answering me because you know what's coming and don't want to face it.

Sometimes I wish more than anything that I never fell for you – and I did, head over heels. I am so afraid of what might happen next. Am I going to lose you? Are we still going to be like brother and sister? Or is something else going to happen? I don't know, and I am terrified to think of some of the outcomes this little episode could result in.

I wish like hell I hadn't sent you that text message. I wish I hadn't fallen in love with you. I wish I would have had the courage to say this to your face. Please answer me, please don't make me lose you if the answer is no, and please tell me, if the answer is no, that you still love me like a sister. I can live with that. I am so sorry I couldn't guard my heart and stop it from falling in love with you.

COMMENTS:

>> Multiple people posted their support.

>> (Update from the original poster 3 days later) Hey. I'm the person who wrote the original regret. First, thank you so much for posting this. I looked at the site this afternoon and burst out crying – I've been holding that in for about three days now. I needed that. So thanks. Second, thanks for the support from everyone. I looked at the comments and started crying again. God, I think this is the first time I've cried in a year ... but thank you. It means a lot to me. Third, he still hasn't answered me. I don't know if he will or not, but I'll tell you if he does. Thank you again for everything.

>> (Update from the original poster 2 weeks later) Well then. To make a very long story short, after sending him about ten texts over two days because I was afraid he'd got in a car accident or something, I got a voicemail from him saying that his PHONE BROKE (oh my goodness) and he couldn't read any of his text messages. Sheesh. So, I told him over the phone. Joy. In a nutshell, he told me (the day before Christmas Eve) that this "wasn't an issue he wanted to resolve over the phone." Oh, great. So we said we'd talk in person at our mutual church's Christmas Eve mass (help) and we did ... and the subject never came up. School has now started back up, and I'm seeing him every day, and apparently neither of us has the guts to bring up the subject. But you know, I think I'm OK with that. I don't want to push him into something, so I think we'll just take it slow. Sometimes the signs are there, sometimes they're not. Even if the answer is no, I tried, right? And I don't think I'm going to lose him as a friend either. That's all I really care about right now.

SECRET REGRET: I don't regret telling our parents you were doing drugs 5 years ago. I don't regret making you feel bad about your coke habit, and have you look into Mom's eyes and see how scared she was. I don't regret it at all.

Because you stopped.

I had to do something, and you were incapable of listening.

Maybe I should have tried harder to reach out to you, but you don't even realize how far gone you were. What I regret the most is knowing that you still occasionally do drugs. And now I don't have the courage to confront you and tell you how much of an idiot I think you are, still doing this.

"You've got it under control" – it's BS!
And you don't tell me about it – I hear it from friends. I regret not being able to just beg you to stop. Do you not realize how scared I am for you? And how all this is affecting our younger brother – he's only 19 and you're his hero. Please just stop being so irresponsible with your life, you are far too important to us! I love you big brother!

F/24

COMMENTS:

>> My sister had a coke problem and committed suicide as a result – believe me, I wish with all my being that I had done more. I live with constant regret. Do everything you can to intervene NOW, before it's too late! There's no such thing as a "casual" coke habit.

SECRET REGRET: If I could go back and change one thing, I would tell. I would tell my school counselor what was happening in my home. I would go to the police and make a report. I would contact social services. Because I didn't and none of my other siblings did either, I am 42 years old and still suffering the effects of post-traumatic stress syndrome. You are dead these past 21 years and I have suffered every single day of it. Torn between the loyalty of a daughter and the love she holds for her father and the hate a victim holds for her attacker.

COMMENTS:

>> I didn't tell either. I still haven't. I'm only 18 but I don't think I'll ever have the courage to say anything. I'm in college to become a psychologist. So maybe I can help others to find the courage I didn't have.

SECRET REGRET: I regret that because of you, my eating disorder has re-surfaced. I hate myself, and it's all your fault. You were a shit best friend anyway, but you didn't have to go this far. You and her. You're sick. I hate you both. But not as much as I hate myself. For not being good enough for him and now, not even you.

P.S. I wish I had sent that text. IT'S TRUE.

COMMENTS:

>> I know exactly how you feel. You are so, so not alone. I'm sorry :(

SECRET REGRET: "If I had a second chance to do ONE thing differently in my life, I would have pulled the trigger twice because the first time and only time I ever loaded and put the gun in my mouth and pulled the trigger, it didn't fire." That was 15 painful years ago. I am now divorced with a son. I hope his life is happy; he is the only reason I am here.

M/39

SECRET REGRET: I regret that I spent the last 8 years feeling sorry for myself and living within my own fear and insecurities rather than being the man she needed me to be.

Perhaps if I had opened my eyes sooner she'd never have loved him, and never would I have to be in this place where we both admit she settled for me, because she couldn't have him, and though I love her more than life, the returned emotion isn't the same from her, and may never be, because I blew it a long time ago.

I only hope now that it isn't too late and I can fix it.

Male, 33

SECRET REGRET: If I could have a second chance, I would not have gone to the store Sept. 26, 2008. I wouldn't have been the one person out of 13,000 to run over a little 2-year-old girl. I wouldn't be the one responsible for her death. I wouldn't be the one having to deal with the emotional upheaval that was created that day. I wouldn't be the one living with the memory of her dying in my arms.

COMMENTS:

>> A terrible thing happened ... it was an unplanned terrible twist of fate but you cannot continue to punish yourself. I assume you are in counseling and if not I would suggest just going and talking to someone. It will hurt for a long time but you will accept/understand it was an accident over time. I hope you have friends and family for support. Best of luck.

SECRET REGRET: I regret never seeing you when you were diagnosed with leukemia. The truth is I was scared to see you like that. Now I miss you and feel ashamed whenever your name is brought up.

SECRET REGRET: I regret being so afraid, I regret thinking I wasn't worth it. I regret hiding behind glasses and sloppy clothes, instead of taking the time to shine, because I didn't think I was pretty enough to try. I regret thinking I was ugly because I'm overweight, instead of showing the world that I am beautiful the way I am.

I regret thinking I wasn't good enough, but I look forward to changing ... starting now.

Female, 19

COMMENTS:

>> Reading this totally shocked me. It was literally like looking at something I had written myself. Good Luck and be happy with your change. I regret that I haven't made it there yet.

SECRET REGRET: I regret giving you my heart when all you wanted was my body. I regret falling for your stupid tricks and your cute little words and somewhere in between falling in love when you didn't feel the same way. I regret letting you in, only to be let down when you stopped talking to me after I poured my heart out. I regret feeling inadequate even though you DON'T deserve me.

COMMENTS:

>> Hang in there. My ex did something similar. He told me he loved me and that he would always be there for me. I made him promise to be with me and only me because I was so young. He promised and I thought he was genuine. He left me. It broke my heart. I thought he really did love me and all he wanted was someone to control and someone to sleep with.

SECRET REGRET: If I could do one thing differently, I would never have kissed him. I would never have allowed him to come over that night. Then he wouldn't have awoken a part of me that I killed a long time ago. We want different things in life. It will never work. Yet I love him like I've never loved another.

Female, 38

SECRET REGRET: I regret that I'm a twin. I hate it that no matter how hard I try, no one really sees us as separate people. I hate it that every time someone likes me, it turns out they were only seeing you in me – you are the one everyone wants to be with and I'm there just because. I hate that we really ARE so similar sometimes that I can't blame anyone and so I have to try to change myself, even when I don't want to. Just so people may eventually recognize that I'm not you. I regret that our friends like you better, think you're smarter, call you more frequently, confide in you, and that it's really my fault because I don't want to have the same friendships you do and yet I love the same people. I want to be that close, but because you are, I won't let myself.

I regret that someone I care about a lot is crossing the country to visit you. And didn't tell me. She's going to say she loves you. I regret that I can never tell either of you this

www.SecretRegrets.com

because I want both of you to be happy and you are more fragile people than I am on the outside. I regret that I can't show emotion because you do, so all that you let others see, I bottle away and hold inside. That's why I regret that I can't express how jealous I am of the relationship you two have when I thought she was the only one who could see us differently because for once, I was the one who was loved. Not anymore, I guess.

But I regret that I can't tell you this because I love you too much.

COMMENTS:

>> It's hard to understand what you mean when you're not a twin. Fortunately for you I am one, and I know exactly what you mean. No matter what you do differently, or how much you try, people always see you as the same as your twin. Most people don't understand that and they think it's easy. It's not. You want to be your own person; you want your own identity, not a shadow. Don't give up being who you are, one day you will find someone who sees you, for you.

>> You sound a lot stronger than your twin, willing to make sacrifices for those you love. Seems like a pretty big difference to me and I'm certain you'll find someone who cherishes that.

SECRET REGRET: I regret that I am the one who has the power. I know where you work and where you live and I know your name. All you know about me is that I am a married woman who you spent time with one night. I know you have forgotten my first name by now. You have no numbers for me. You don't know anything about me. Why do I regret this? Because I want you in a way that I have never wanted any other man before and I spend so much time imagining that I will see you in places that you will never be and imagining words you will never say to me and imagining things between us that never were between us. I regret this because I felt really "wanted" on that one night and that is something that I have not felt in a long time and I really want that again. Who wouldn't want that again?

COMMENTS:

>> You are not alone. I have that same regret.

>> As do I :o(

SECRET REGRET: I regret not being in your life after high school.

I regret the fact that now, almost 5 years later, you're both dying from cystic fibrosis.

I regret your mom telling us you weren't up for visitors.

I regret knowing YOU are deteriorating faster then your twin brother.

I'm regretting this now because I know you will not be up for visitors anytime soon.

I also know you will not make it to the end of the summer.

You are 23. You have been given a week.

I hate the disease that is robbing you of your life.

I'm sorry I couldn't do more but write this stupid regret.

I miss you.

I miss who you were. I miss everything about you.

22/f

SECRET REGRET: If I had a second chance I would not have had a retaliation affair. When I confronted you about stepping outside of our marriage you were horrified, and did everything possible to try and make amends, even marriage counseling. I couldn't bring myself to forgive you. I wanted you to experience the same indescribable pain that you had caused me. So, I cheated while I was on a week long vacation with friends. I am so ashamed of myself, and don't think I will ever be able to tell you. I should have just left things as they were. I feel worse now than before I strayed. This wasn't a victory. I didn't get the smug satisfaction I thought that I would by sleeping with another man.

Married Female 32

SECRET REGRET: I regret that I am so selfish that I am not willing to be the one who has to change. It should be me. But instead I pray every night for my husband to fall in love with someone else and leave me, or for the man who loves me to realize we can never be together and just stop loving me.

COMMENTS:

\>> I didn't write this, but I certainly could have.

\>> I didn't write this either, but I, too, could have ...

SECRET REGRET: If I had a second chance, I'd risk more. I've lived a safe, comfortable, life. I have a safe, comfortable home in a safe, comfortable town. If I had a second chance, I'd go on that trip, take the job far away, run faster and try harder.

Female, 29

SECRET REGRET: I regret being happy and excited. If I would've known you would be laying on the snowy highway dead less that two hours later, I would have dropped to my knees and wept. I no longer like school closings. I no longer like snow or flashing red lights. I miss you and your special smile and I am sorry I didn't say goodbye. I also regret that you are slowly fading. It's been over a year and your face is starting to get fuzzy and your voice no longer brings a smile to my face when I am upset. I think about you every day, but you are slowly leaving. My psych doctor said it was normal, but I feel horrible that I can no longer remember the exact spot of your dimples and it kills me. I miss you and love you.

Female/15

COMMENTS:

\>> I'm so sorry for your loss. I'm sorry that this happened to you, and I will be thinking of you. It is horrible, but it does get easier. It's been three years, and I can't remember his smell, but the memories never fade. I hope for you that you can get the help you need. Keep fighting. <3

\>> I'm so sorry): I know exactly how you feel, I still find myself going into shops and smelling his aftershave just to find some way to make myself remember, it's been two and a half years, and I hate myself more each day for forgetting the simple things I should.

SECRET REGRET: I regret not punching you in the face when I had the chance. Then you would have something to complain about. Does it make you feel like a man when you put down our mother and follow her around town in your car just to degrade her? I regret losing a brother, but I will never regret losing such a miserable human being.

SECRET REGRET: If I had a second chance, I never would have said those things to you. I wanted to hurt you and I knew exactly what to say. I never thought I would be that cruel. I'm so sorry. I know you've said you forgive me, but I can't really forgive myself.

And just for the record, you are not stupid, and you are not ugly, and you are not a whore. I love you so much and you are beautiful inside and out.

COMMENTS:

>> I don't know who left this post ... but I know who I wish it were. If it is you ... I want you to know how much this means to me. And that I forgive you.

SECRET REGRET: If I had a second chance, I would have told you I was interested in you. I don't care if I get discharged anymore. Being alone is too much and I can't take it anymore.

I hate that I have to keep this all to myself. I hate that I won't ever know if you shared the same feelings as I did. I hate that I can't be myself because of a stupid job. Maybe if circumstances were different we could of had something but now all I am left with are what-if's.

I will always remember the night we met and the drunken nights where we always ended up in each other's arms.

21/male

COMMENTS:

>> I'm sorry that you're in a job, probably the most important job our country has to offer, and you can't be honest. You make me proud every single day. You make me proud because you are you.

SECRET REGRET: If I had a second chance, I would not have been so promiscuous in high school and college. Now that I'm married it is so weird to run into those people. It seems like it was another lifetime, but still, people remember that about me. It's not as much fun now as it was at the time. I realize what a joke I must have been. It doesn't matter why I was that way. I wish I could tell everyone that I'm bipolar and how that affected me and who I was then. They would not understand anyway. I just wish I could have had a "normal" life. Those stupid decisions have long lasting effects that I will never be able to change.

SECRET REGRET: I regret not appreciating what you did for me. My whole life started with you, and all I could do was call you a bitch and talk shit about you to my friends so they all hated you too ... I'm sorry I hurt you, embarrassed you, and pushed you away ... It's been years since we've said I love you. We aren't close at all ...

I should have been a better daughter. I shouldn't have made drinking and my friends more important than my family. I haven't told you in almost 10 years, but I love you mom, so much.

F/21

COMMENTS:

>> Honey, I love you too ... never forget that. Just come home.

>> Tell her now, you are still so young. It may not feel like it, but you still have a lifetime to tell her how much you love her.

SECRET REGRET: I regret that I don't have the courage. Everyday I see you. I walk up behind you and slowly revise the words I want to say. But as soon as you turn around I walk away, as if I was never going to speak to you. Why can't I just do it? Why can't I just talk to you? I know your name ... but you don't know mine.

There's some just something about this boy that I can't get over.

F/15

SECRET REGRET: If I had a second chance in my life, I would be the daughter that my parents have always wanted. I would be their perfect first born, instead of the messed up practice child that always does everything wrong. I would change it all just for them to accept me and love me as their daughter.

COMMENTS:

>> Don't think for a second that you let your parents down. Sure you may think that they think you're just a messed up child, but they probably love you. Even with all the "mess ups" you made.

SECRET REGRET: You read this every day, since I sent you the link a while ago. I've always thought about posting, but never really had the guts.

But tonight, I wanted to tell you my regret.

It's probably nothing compared to the stories of others but I wish you could see it, and tell it's me writing.

I regret not being able to hug you.
You tell me "we just don't hug" but I always hate myself when you feel sad, or angry and I can't seem to comfort you other than with words.

I just wish I could be a better friend and give you the hope and comfort that you need, especially now, when everything seems to be on your mind.

I'm trying my hardest to break that barrier down even more and hug you without awkwardness. I hope I don't regret anything else about our friendship. Ever.

Female/17

SECRET REGRET: The biggest regret that I have in my life is that I didn't decide to work from home on September 11, 2001, like I was supposed to. I was originally supposed to take additional time to complete a project for the company I was working for. I completed my work in the early evening on the 10th because I knew that since I was the ranking member in my department, my boss was on vacation, and my colleague was in an all-day meeting, that the staff needed a full-time managerial presence at the office.

I was in the World Trade Center when the first plane hit. I was trampled on in the rush to get out of the building complex. I saw bodies throw themselves from the North Tower, and I saw the second plane hit the South Tower. I was never the same man again. I now suffer from Acute PTSD and am on disability. My mental and physical health is failing as a result. I have many regrets in my life, but this is one do over I'd gladly have.

COMMENTS:

>> I lost my cousin and my sister that day. I was so caught up in all the people that died that I never thought of the survivors ... thanks for changing my perspective.

SECRET REGRET: I would have left my ex sooner to really find out who I was. Now I know, but it would have been great to get here quicker.

COMMENTS:

>> At least you had the courage to do it.

SECRET REGRET: I regret that when he asked me, I said yes ... because I was too afraid of hurting his feelings to tell him otherwise. My feelings for him had recently changed and I didn't know why. I hoped it would just be a phase and I would fall back in love with him. Now it's almost a year later, we have a condo, a ring, and a wedding in 7 months. I am terrified that I will never be happy with him, but I can't stand the thought of losing him because I am more terrified of hurting him and ending up alone.

COMMENTS:

>> You owe him the truth. Things get worse after marriage so don't think anything different will happen if you don't love him now. Free yourself and him.

>> You will never forgive yourself if you don't do something about it now. I would have done the same thing years ago if asked, and am thankful every day I was able to break it off and find my soul mate.

>> You must tell him the truth and find someone else. A condo and a wedding are just things that can be sold or cancelled; a life in deceit and self-hatred is much harder to fix. Please, for his sake, and your own, leave him before it gets too difficult ... I know this from first hand experience, and it will only lead to trouble down the road.

>> You have to leave him for both of your sakes. I didn't and here I am 10 years later full of regrets, the difference is I love him but am not IN love with him. We stopped having sex 4 years ago, we are basically roommates and I am only 40. Please be honest with yourself and him!

>> You have my regret except I married him. Leave before you get married. It's just that much harder after. I know because I'm working on it. I'm looking into the divorce and another place to live. I knew I wasn't in love with him before we got married but I was too afraid to cancel the wedding. I was too worried about what everyone else would think and having to find another place to live. I thought I wasn't sure if it really was because I wasn't in love with him or some other more "normal" reason (i.e., "just give it time"). I would tell you to just do it already. Just leave. It's better for everyone that way. But I know how hard it is to "just leave." You know what you have to do. You don't need everyone else to tell you. Just ... don't wait too long. It only gets harder.

SECRET REGRET: I regret that I started cutting myself over two years ago, and that I had stopped for so long only to start again in college. I regret that I am so hard on myself when things don't work out, and that I let it affect me so deeply. I regret losing touch with the only people who used to help me, that I let my support structure go and that I don't open up to my new friends. I hate that I lash out against my physical self because it's all I think I have ... I don't know what I'd do if I wasn't attractive. I regret losing the strong and loving person I used to be.

Male 18

COMMENTS:

>> You can still save yourself. Don't give up and torture yourself like this. You'll get through it; you just have to be strong. F/17

>> You are stronger than you think. When you feel like all is lost, look deep inside yourself for hope ... you WILL be ok ... I promise.

>> There is hope still. I have been free for 64 months this month. There are days that are struggles but there is hope. There will come a day that things will change for you – don't look for it. Don't pressure yourself to stop – just let it happen. ::hugs::

>> For five years I went through this. I haven't in about a year. Every day is a struggle but I fight it. Be strong – I know you can! The day will come when you can walk away from the pain. Try writing everything down in a journal. It has worked for me. Exercise is great relief as well.

SECRET REGRET: I regret that I miss you, and smile when I get the chance to see you. I regret that your words haunt me, and probably always will. "You're not worth loving." Those words have dictated my life. I regret most that I still want your approval.

But Daddy, I will never regret loving you.

20/F

COMMENTS:

>> I was shocked when I got to the last line of your regret. Absolutely awful. No child should ever, EVER have to hear that from a parent. He does not deserve to be your father; you deserve much better in a dad. You are only 20. I hope you can somehow put him away and move on to have a good life. God bless.

>> It blows me away that adults can treat children that way. You are a treasure, even if they didn't have the sense to treasure you.

>> Growing up I was constantly put down by my grandmother who told me daily how fat, ugly, stupid, and worthless I was. She told me I would have to try to be smart, because I'd never be pretty and nobody would ever love me. The physical abuse was pretty irrelevant compared to the constant tearing down. It seemed reinforced by the fact that she always told my sister how beautiful she was, how much potential she had for a great future. How talented she was. Enrolling her in modeling school, taking her to photo shoots and acting auditions. (I was the one who wanted to act, but grandma said nobody would want me on their TV.) I regret believing her. I have spent the last 20 years trying to overcome that programming, hating anyone who "pretended" to like me (because obviously it couldn't be true), hurting people who cared for me because I couldn't believe in or trust them. Years later I finally talked to my sister about our childhood and found out we both grew up resenting the other. She got pushed into most of the things I wanted to do and I was jealous because she actually had those opportunities. Meanwhile, she was jealous of me because I never got bullied or harassed into activities and such. Neither of us ever saw the abuse that the other went through. She never knew how I was constantly put down for being ugly and worthless. I had no idea that she was being told, literally, to use her body to get what she wanted from life. I regret taking so many years to talk to her and find these things out, because we both could've started healing sooner. However. We've grown up. We've moved on. We will dance on that bitch's grave when she finally dies.

SECRET REGRET: If I had a second chance, I would have quit my job when my children were born. I would have not made so many excuses to say, "I have to work." Because they were mostly lies. Lies told, because honestly, the weeks I did spend at home scared me to death. It was easier to hire someone to Mother them, and pay her to do my job.

I would have not made excuses for only nursing my babies for a few months. I would have told my husband and my friends and my mother-in-law that I would raise my children. The heck with what they "wanted" or "expected" or thought I should do. My mother-in-law, although very nasty about the fact that I "worked," was more than happy to take my kids on weekends, when I was more than happy to be "so tired" to raise them myself. My husband and I broke up anyway, as our lives diverged, and without family time to hold us together, we were just spending money, and making excuses for not being with our children.

But I was too obsessed with "my life" and how I thought I was supposed to live it. Make money, have fun, be everything to all people, except those who really should mean the most to me. I was selfish, and self-absorbed. I wish I could go back (hysterectomy and now I can't have any more kids, and they are getting older) and make the difference when it counts.

Now my children have no time for me. At first I was angry, but I understand. I always made excuses as to why I never had time for them. Or took them on a few errands and told people we were taking Quality Time. All BS. It was about me then.

Now, it's too late. They have their own lives and as my ex and I "worked" all the time, our children learned to get comfort elsewhere. They expect us to pay for school, which we are doing, and to lend them money, which we do, but it is an artifact of our poor self-absorbed parenting that we feel we have to give them things and money, instead of giving them our time, when we had the chance.

I wish I could change the past. I'd have my children, say the heck with the huge house, and the big screen TV, and the new car every few years, and the vacations, the expensive food, the eating out, the business suits I thought I "needed," the radical shoes, I "needed" lunch out every day, and the cost of day care. None of which was necessary. I would stop all the excuses, say "NO" to spending money on anything but the essentials, forget the BS that I "deserved" what I earned for myself, and spend my time at home and BEING with my children.

Now, their only concerns are what my ex and I can do for them. And, I realize they do this because we bought what we thought was love for too long.

I hope they can be with their children, but I am afraid the pattern will continue.

So, we open the checkbook, instead of our hearts.

SECRET REGRET: I regret that when we were young I didn't see how much you really loved me. I never imagined that after all the hurt I caused you that you could still feel anything for me. I regret that you never let me know that you still loved me and still wanted to be with me, because I always loved you and wanted to be with you as well. I regret that I was too scared to think that I still had a chance with you after all I had done. If either of us had taken the risk, told the other how we still felt, we would be together now. We would have had more than 25 years of happiness together, instead of being married to other people. You once asked me, "What if there was more than one road to happiness?" I know that you are right. We would have been so happy together. We are each other's first love and we love each other still, 30 years later, just as strongly. I regret that we did not try harder and will never know what could have been.

COMMENTS:

>> I didn't write this, but I could have and I should have. My biggest regret is how I treated my first true love. At a time when she needed someone to care for her, to show her how good people were capable of being. I didn't. My selfishness and narcissism outweighed any ability I had to be true, and trustworthy and loyal. I regret not recognizing true love. I regret putting my needs above hers. I regret letting her down. I regret not being the man then I am capable of being now. I envy those with more than one path to happiness; my path was laid out 28 years ago. I regret making the selfish choice and not choosing what I now know is true love.

SECRET REGRET: I wish that you would just hold me again. Marriage is hard, and you and I seem to be loosing the battle. I wish that you would make love to me like you used to. I wish that I didn't feel alone, and that I didn't feel like I needed to go get affection from someone else to be happy. I wish your medication allowed you to touch me again ... I wish I had never had to hospitalize you because you lost your touch with reality. I remember what we used to be like, before you lost reality. I miss you, even though I see you every day. I feel like I lost my husband that day in May ... and gained a stranger that I am forced to love. I miss you soo much.

COMMENTS:

>> Wow! I don't know you but my heart aches for you. Hope things work out soon. All the best. I will be praying for you.

SECRET REGRET: If I had a second chance I would have told you I had a crush on you in high school. Five years later we have reconnected and I think you might be the one. We live 600 miles apart and I am afraid our chance has passed. It breaks my heart to know what she did to you. I always hoped I would be your first and only true love. Stealing away weekends is well worth it for me but it isn't enough. What could have happened if I would have said something 5 years ago?

F 23

SECRET REGRET: I would have stopped "dreaming" and started "doing" long ago.

SECRET REGRET: If I had a second chance, I would have never allowed myself to rack up so much credit card debt. Tens of thousands of dollars later, I'm on the edge of losing it all. And nobody knows this but me. From the outside, all appears normal in my life. This burden is like a ticking time bomb. I have to fix it before it blows up in my face and ruins my life and my family's.

COMMENTS:

>> I'm sorry, but trust that everything will be ok if you seek help – don't try to carry this burden alone, and don't bury your head in the sand. There are people who can help you, professional and personal, and more importantly the pressure on you will be lessened. Money is important but never more than your health.

SECRET REGRET: I regret pretending not to notice you loved me in high school.
I regret not filling out the application to go to the same college as you.
I regret choosing not to listen when you came to my show at my college to tell me you loved me ... with flowers.
I regret not leaving with you when you came to my wedding to stop it.
I regret using you as the rebound guy during/after my divorce.

I regret falling completely in love with you.
I regret all the times I tried to prove you made a mistake by ending it.
I regret that I can't fall out of love with you.
But most of all,
I regret letting you ruin every other shot at love I have had.
And I would regret writing this if you ever read it, and realized it was me.
Female/ 27

COMMENTS:

\>> You don't have to regret these things. You can move on to better things in life. If he doesn't realize he lost a great person, then you have to stop worrying and move on. It'll be ok in the end =)

SECRET REGRET: I regret not being the perfect guy that you deserved. You were and are my everything. We met three years ago and shared a whole world together. I gave you everything I had, my honor, my wealth, my respect, and my time, but I still fell short. Most importantly, I gave you my love. I loved you and still love you with all my heart. I regret not trying to find you after you said you did not want to see me anymore. Now, you have started to move on to bigger and better things. I still pray for your happiness and contentment, with or without me. I just wish you hadn't given me up so suddenly and so easily. I miss your breath, your touch, and your smile. Most importantly, I miss the kindness in your eyes, and the smile that brightened even the darkest clouds. I love you, my everything. I regret not becoming the prince you totally deserve.

18/M

COMMENTS:

\>> Any girl would give her heart for a guy she cared about to write such things about her. Even at nearly 30 I'm still looking for that kind of love.

\>> That was the nicest thing I've ever read, I was crying about 10 seconds after reading it. I really hope someone loves me one day the way you loved your girlfriend.

\>> That girl would be extremely lucky to have you. She shouldn't have given you up because she'll never get anyone better.

www.SecretRegrets.com

>> ARE YOU REAL? DATE ME. DAMN.

>> In five years you'll realize exactly how insane this post is. Until then, just remember that even if she was one in a million, there are about 6777 more of her out there …

SECRET REGRET: If I had a second chance, I would've tried to do even more to stop your drug and alcohol use. You were everyone's best friend, an 18 year old, graduated with straight A's, ready for college, so many friends and family that loved and supported you. Two jobs, your own car, and your beautiful eyes, features and strong physique. So athletic.

I would've tried even harder to make you see the road you were choosing was so destructive and how your choice of new friends had gone wrong. I would've insisted that you get help for substance abuse. I would've taken you to church more often. I would've insisted you go with me to Mom and Dad's more often to spend more time with the grandparents that loved you so much.

You were the perfect only son for me who I loved more than anything in this world. I would go back to that night that your life ended and made you stay at home. At least perhaps that one night would've resulted in your reconsideration of your life and the consequences of partying. That the consequences went so much further than just your life. Your life, ended by one needle stick with Heroin, has shattered the lives of all of our family. We all loved you so much. I would've done everything all over again to try to make you see things from a different perspective.

Male, 45

COMMENTS:

>> The same thing happened to me and my brother. Addicts only change when they're ready to. Most never are. Please don't torture yourself like that. If you loved him and he knew it, then you did everything you possibly could.

>> Wow. That made me cry. I'm an ex-addict. Still alive.

SECRET REGRET: If I had a second chance, I wouldn't have let you leave her. She was the closet thing to a mom I ever had. We were so happy, the five of us. You and I hate each other now. She and I still love each other. If you two hadn't broken up you wouldn't be dating someone 2 years older than me. And I wouldn't be living in San Francisco because I can't bear to be associated with your life style.

I already lost one parent. I wish I hadn't had to lose both.

I miss you Dad, I hope one day you wake up and realize I'm missing from your life and you want me back. 'Cause if you'd ask I'd be there in a heartbeat.

SECRET REGRET: If I was given a chance to do ONE thing differently in my life ... I would never have been such a bitch to you in high school.

The reality of what the words, the exclusion, the pettiness did to you never quite hit home until a friend of yours told me years later. Now it haunts me.

Truthfully, I don't know what's worse – that I did it, or that I didn't realize it until I was told. I am so sorry. If there is anyone I wish happiness for it's you, and I do, SO much. Whenever anyone mentions you, when I go home I cry a little inside and feel a shame like you could never know.

I don't want to ever apologize to you though, because I know you'll forgive me and that will be worse.

Female, 24

COMMENTS:

>> I really think you should apologize. I can assure you it will mean the world to the person you hurt and it will help you.

SECRET REGRET: I regret living a lie for almost a year, even though I know I would be happier without you, I stick around for the kids' sake and fear of the unknown. The other problem is that you know I am intimate with someone else and you seem to be okay with that idea, as long as I don't leave ¬— but I love him, not you.

When our youngest graduates high school, I will be finishing my Master's degree and leaving. I count the days until my life will be free of the overbearing, controlling relationship I've been forced to remain in for over 10 years. 709 days remaining, and I will be free from you and ready to start my new life.

35/F

COMMENTS:

>> Mom? Is that you?

>> I applaud you for staying for your child. You are a strong woman.

>> Leave him NOW. Your kids aren't oblivious to the fact that you're miserable, I can assure you. And the unknown is always scary, but it couldn't be any worse than what you're dealing with already. So do everyone a favor and start your new life NOW.

>> Same thing going on here, but it's down to one year now ... Scary, but the planning has begun! It's a lot easier to live with someone you don't really like sometimes, when you know you're leaving. Good luck!!!

>> He doesn't know it, but I am on my way out. Even though I haven't even finished my associate's and have a minimum-wage job, I will scrape and save and be out in 3 months, and he'll have no idea where I, or our daughter, live. She's not even three years old yet, but I can already see the hostility affecting who she will become. I love her too much to let her watch me accept the way he treats me and think that is the way a man treats a woman he loves. And the man that I actually love? Well, we'll most likely never be together, because he's staying in a marriage he doesn't want to be in, at least until his son turns 18.

>> Your kids see the unhappiness in both of you, whether you knowingly show it or not. Dragging it out helps no one.

SECRET REGRET: If I had a second chance I would never have been bullied by my mother into the relationship, which resulted in my first marriage, because it was abusive. HE was abusive. If I had a second chance I would never have married him.

If by some random freak of nature I HAD married him, if I had a second chance I would have left him the first time he strayed – three weeks after our wedding. Because allowing him to get away with being a lying, cheating scumbag paved the way for years of him being a lying, cheating scumbag.

A happy P.S. I met him at 15, married him at 21, and left him at 30. I met the love of my life when I was 40. HE was worth the wait!!!

COMMENTS:

>> I am 42 years of age (never married) and still waiting for my prince. It is nice to hear about the sweet endings after years of turmoil.

>> Met my ex at 15, married at 21, left him at 27. Even 5 years after the divorce my parents tried to tell me I belonged with HIM! NOT. Now I'm 35 and have also met the love of my life. He's 24 so of course, my parents don't really approve, but hey who cares this is MY life and I'm finally starting to live it! I'm so glad to hear it can work out for some of us ... Kudos to you, may you have all the love beauty & light you can handle in life!

SECRET REGRET: If I had a second chance I would have done it.

I would have joined Americorps, or taught English in Japan, or driven across the country with a friend, it doesn't really matter what "it" is. It's more what I wouldn't have done. I wouldn't have chosen what I knew over what could be. I would have been brave instead of seeking comfort. I would have left a relationship that was leaving me anyway.

Now I wonder what could have been. Where I could have gone, what I could have done, who I could have been, what I might have accomplished. Mostly I wonder if I'd have a better sense of myself if I'd given myself the chance to explore the world and compare, instead of staying in the place I knew to become stagnant.

Now all I can do is move forward and urge others to do the same. Funny thing, I don't regret anything I've done, even the mistakes. Just the things I didn't. When presented with a "should I do it?" moment, please say, "yes." Do it. Do it well. Don't look back.

Female/33

COMMENTS:

>> I chose to do it all ... and now I wonder what I left behind ... life is always a Catch-22. You are where you are for a reason. You would not be you if anything had been different.

>> Is this Gina?

>> Not Gina. I do more than I should. My only regret is taking on too much.

>> You're 33, lady! Do it all now! Why regret what you can do now?

SECRET REGRET: If I had a second chance, I would never have allowed myself to be drawn into anorexia. This eating disorder has taken over my life to the point where I'm starving myself for three months and then binging and purging for three weeks straight. I have f'd up every organ in my body. I've been so busy counting calories and restricting that I've never hung out with friends. I don't even have any close friends anymore, let alone a boyfriend. I'm 5'10" and I weigh 98 pounds. I used to be attractive and was told that I had a great personality. Look at me now. No friends, no life, no happiness, no meaning. I'm trying so hard to look at food as an energy source and not as a big fat molecule ready to take over my body. But I can't. Even if I try to eat a "snack," it will activate a binge. And then a binge turns into more binges, and pretty soon, I'll be throwing up all over my damned carpet.

I want to live normally, but I can't. I want to be normal, to think normally and to love myself.

I can't.

Someone save me.

Female, 19

COMMENTS:

>> Awwwwww Sweetie! I've been where you're at and you can get better. My heart aches for you little one. I was 16 when I found that awful life-taking disease. I was scared and alone for so long, then when I was 20, a doctor finally took me under his wings and saved my life. Life hasn't been easy I have to tell you this but I found things in life that mean so much more to me now than then. I know the pain of not having control of my life and feeling like nothing matters anymore. The pain does go away and life does seep in if you just let it. Life can be so sweet and wonderful. It took me a long time to realize that. I wasn't as lucky as you to be able to reach out on the internet. And I'm so thankful for that these days. You can find the help and realize you're not alone. We are here for you. We understand more than you know. You don't walk down that road alone. There are so many of us that understand. Just reach out and get help. It's there, and there is such a wonderful reward when you do get better. The reward is a wonderful, exciting world for you to explore. I let myself get better and now I'm going to be 44 in three weeks. I'm a mother and a grandmother and life just couldn't be sweeter. I'm sending you much love and all the hugs you can handle!

>> Been there ... done that. It takes A LOT to realize it's not what you think. I am 34 ... and just getting it. Please believe me when I say YOU CAN KICK ITS ASS ... just keep trying. It's worth it.

SECRET REGRET: I regret that this world is full of pricks. I regret that I can't seem to shut them up. I regret the fact people don't care for anyone but themselves.
I regret my way of thinking about the future at times. I regret a lot of things. I regret the fact I still don't feel like I'm good enough for you. M/16

COMMENTS:

>> I'm sure you are good enough for her, go for it. She's probably thinking about you right now. Text her, ring her. I'm waiting on a guy to do the same for me. He may not think I'm too good for him, but I can always hope. I love hearing from him. His phone calls and texts leave me smiling all day long. I miss him.

>> You said it perfectly. I'm just sad you realized this at such a young age. You shouldn't have to feel this way yet.

SECRET REGRET: I wish I'd just told you to go to hell. I feel like such a coward now, and I still think you're a BITCH.

SECRET REGRET: If I could do one thing differently, I would go back in time and spend more time with you. Of course, it would be better if I could go back in time, knowing what I know now – that you weren't as healthy as we thought you were – and fix things so that you would still be with us today. But that's not possible.

Now I'll never be able to run to see you when you get home from work again. I'll never be able to sit next to you while we watch American Idol again. I'll never be able to show you my art and see how proud you are of me again. I'll never get to talk to you about music and movies – thanks for always acting like I had good taste, it's kind of embarrassing looking back on it. I'll never get to go on a bike ride with you again. I'll never get to get up extra early to eat breakfast with you again. I'll never get to hug and kiss you goodnight again.

Listing all these things makes it sound like we spent so much time together, but we could have spent more. I was always glued to the computer, or doing some other pointless thing that doesn't matter now. And now I'll never get to be Daddy's little girl again.

COMMENTS:

>> Thank you so much for this ... it has made me realize that we do get caught up in little things that don't even matter.

>> Thank you for this, because I will now go on and call my father, maybe even see him again. It has been over a year since I've seen him. Our time here together is so limited, and so precious. Thank you!

SECRET REGRET: If I had a second chance at anything, I wouldn't have fought so hard against the help that would've changed my life. I wasted so much time and so much effort to deny that I was sick and to justify my behavior, instead of using that effort to work toward actually getting better.

If I had spent half the energy I used to stay sick, to work with the therapists, psychologists, and psychiatrists, I wouldn't be so close to death right now. If I had accepted their help, I would be healthy and happy today. Instead, I'm still fighting for my life. I'm so sorry that I wasted so much time.

I want nothing more than to be healthy, but I know that I don't deserve that after I spent so long denying the help.

Female/18

COMMENTS:

>> You still are with us. Do what you need to do to get better. Call those you have hurt and just say sorry, and if they REALLY love you they will take it and won't ask for more other than a hug. Hang in there – you will make it, and better late than never. You have already accomplished a lot by realizing that you need help. I wish my husband would do the same for himself, for his son and for me ... but it won't happen. But you, you will be fine I know it. Be happy that you opened your eyes and that you are embarking in a new ship, and that wherever it takes you will be a better place just because you finally helped yourself. And those who are not with you now, who have turned their backs on you ... well maybe they didn't deserve you, and never loved you that much to be able to be there now.

SECRET REGRET: I regret leaving everything I'd worked so hard for at a time in my life when I needed it the most, to move somewhere where I had nothing. I left a great job, in a great city, with family and friends nearby to move to OH where I had none of that. Because of this, I spent the second half of my first pregnancy lonely, miserable, and depressed. I wish I'd had the guts to tell him to leave without me because now I am stuck somewhere that I don't want to be, with people I don't want to be around. I have ended up doing things that I said I wouldn't do in life. I ended up pregnant before being married, got married because I was pregnant, and am married to someone I don't love. I regret ever meeting him and I wish I had a time machine to go back 10 years and change things.

COMMENTS:

>> It's never to late to turn things around. I wish I'd had someone to tell me that a little sooner. I'm

34 and I just moved across the country, got a job that isn't the best and I'm living in an apartment less than half the size of my old house. BUT, I have my friends, my family, and all the opportunity in the world. And for the first time in a very long time, I'm completely happy. Do whatever it takes to get back to where you want to be.

SECRET REGRET: If I had a second chance to do ONE thing differently in my life, I would not change a single thing because I am constantly growing, and without my experiences I would not be who I am.

I am coming through a time anyone would agree is a low time in my life. At first glance I think, oh yes, I would change this and that ... but with more contemplation I realize it has all been perfect.

The abuse, the injuries, the cancer, all the pain and suffering were really perfect. Without my negative experiences I might have been just bouncing along so wrapped up in my thoughts and my ego that I missed what is really important: loving myself and serving others.

Oh and let's remember the past is just a thought. All there ever is, is this beautiful, amazing, perfect moment right now.

Male - Age 41

SECRET REGRET: I used to regret that I wasn't a good enough friend for you. I used to regret not being cool enough or pretty enough for you to call me a "friend" in school.

But now I know better.

I regret regretting those things.

Now, I hope you have something to regret.

Because, the truth is, I AM pretty enough, I AM cool enough, and I AM good enough.

I just hope you open your eyes before you blindly push every single important person out of your life and end up all alone.

-From that girl you knew, ignored, and will never forget.

COMMENTS:

>> Ironically this was posted on my birthday. And ironically I had the same realization. The guy I was in love with and let go is pushing everyone out of his life for his new girlfriend. I miss him way more than I should. Thank you for posting what I wish I could say.

SECRET REGRET: I don't regret having given you permission to end your life ... I still feel that I was right to give you strength in knowing that your friends and loved ones would forgive and understand that you couldn't allow yourself to linger and make them suffer with you for the final stages of AIDS.

I do regret not having been there for you more in the months between when we had the conversation and when you did it.

Most of all I regret that it's been just over a year and I haven't kept my promise to tell our friend how much you loved her and wished you could have been a man with a future, one who could give her the life that she deserves with a white picket fence and fat babies and all the rest.

Every day I try to write that e-mail, or figure out in my head how to say it to her, but my eyes go blurry with tears and I just can't find the words. What if she felt the same way, and letting her know what she could've had, if things were different, hurts her as much as it hurt you knowing that it could never happen?

How do you tell a girl that her best friend loved her most of their lives, but didn't realize it until he'd already done the things that made it impossible to offer her more than pain and suffering?

It's been just over a year and still I have no words. As much as I fear that knowing will hurt her, I fear even more for HIS sake that it won't.

He'll never know how she felt and whether she would regret the missed chance, but I think if I found out she never cared it would break my heart.

31/f

COMMENTS:

>> In my opinion his wishes should be respected. If she didn't feel that way about him, she still cared very much about him in a different way. And if she did feel that way about him, then maybe she can now move on knowing that he felt the same so SHE isn't the one always wondering. I'm sorry for your loss, everything will improve. Have no regrets.

>> I admire your wisdom in not telling the person. Your friend could only really react in two ways: either knowing would depress her, or she would not care. If the former, then this person's true intent would not be realized, because I am sure he never meant her any harm. If she doesn't care, then that would only hurt you more. I would say don't worry about it. I am sure your friend is healing and to reopen that wound would not be wise nor compassionate.

SECRET REGRET: If I had a second chance to do one thing differently in my life, I wouldn't have laid down for my class to walk all over me, because it still affects me today. But now I know that I am so much more than a weird fifth grader with chipmunk cheeks.

And I wish I could go back and tell myself that.

SECRET REGRET: I regret being a curious child and looking through your closet for that favorite pair of shoes you would always hide from me. Not only did I find those shoes but also letters that now make me question whether or not you cheated on my father.

COMMENTS:

>> Things may be what they seem ... but they are often not. Give her the benefit of the doubt. Ask her.

SECRET REGRET: If I had a "second chance" I would never have let my search for my "real father" consume me. It blinded me to what I already had. A real father. I'm so sorry. If there wasn't 15 years of hate on my part toward you, I would tell you I'm sorry, I love you, and thank you for being a real father to a boy who wanted one so badly. You're amazing. To me and my mother, which is something he couldn't do. What's worse is you have always been so nice about EVERYTHING. That makes it hard for me to be anywhere around you, only because I know my feelings are unjust. I'm sorry. I constantly think of ways to make it up to you, things to do to make up for my anger. I just can never go through with them. I don't want you to be angry. I don't want you to know how I really feel because if I were to lose you ... the only father figure that I ever had, the only male that means anything to me ... I'm not sure if I could handle that. So I keep up my lies, and it kills me every time.

COMMENTS:

>> It's never too late to tell someone you love them. Do you really want him to die not knowing that you loved him?

>> It's never too late. If he has been a good father figure to you, he deserves to know it. Otherwise he might be posting on this website regretting that he didn't do enough to gain your love and respect.

SECRET REGRET: I regret spending so much time trying to prove I'm worth something by working so hard on my career. Now that I'm successful, I realize how little time I spent taking care of myself, my health, and my personal life. Now that I know I'm worth something, all I have to show for it are letters after my name.

COMMENTS:

>> I'm working my butt off to gain those letters after my unwed, childless, and otherwise unworthy name.

SECRET REGRET: I regret that I have lived my life in such a way that my mother loves me more than anything, and yet does not like me at all. I regret that I'm not what you wanted. You always ask why I can't finish things I do, and it's because I just want to find the one thing I can do to make you proud, Mom.

Female, 16

COMMENTS:

>> I completely understand. I am 38 years old and have never done anything well enough to make my mother proud of me. I am hoping for the day I stop trying and stop caring.

>> This could have come from my daughter. She used to communicate so well and now she just grunts, hisses and glares. Kind of hard to understand anything when it isn't communicated to you whatsoever. Just giving you a mom's view of this. Plus, not sure how to convey being proud of a child who continues making piss-poor decisions and expects a pat on the back for those as well. Uh, no comment.

SECRET REGRET: I regret taking that bottle of pills last November.

I regret waking up in the hospital with them telling me that I needed to be sent to a special hospital.

I regret that long week. I hated that place. Those girls. Those doctors. Those groups. Those beds. Those showers.

After all of this, most of all, I regret telling my social worker that my dad was innocent and was not the cause.

He was.

17/F

COMMENTS:

>> I am a young doctor and psychiatrist in training. I really hope you will be honest with yourself,

and with your doctors and get the help you need. Your doctors have spent their entire lives and unfathomable amounts of money just to be able to help you. They need you to be honest and open in order to facilitate their being able to help you to the fullest extent. Please do so. And get hooked up with a therapist and possibly a social worker. Minimizing and suppressing will only extend and increase your hurt.

>> Oh sweetie, don't you ever give up on yourself. You are stronger than you think and I pray that you will take the wonderful advice above, because you deserve it. You owe it to yourself to take that scary leap and admit that you need to talk to someone, whether it is public or private. Don't go this alone ... there is always a better way. No more pills.

SECRET REGRET: If I could change one thing, I would have gotten on that plane. I would have gone away with you even if it meant losing my job. I would have gone away with the clothes I had on my back because all that would have truly mattered was the fact that I was with you. The loss of a job doesn't compare to the pain I feel right now, each day, knowing that I've lost you. Jobs can be found. But love, once love is lost, it can't be gained back.

People, all around me, tell me it's "fixable" however you say it's not. I shut my eyes each day and imagine what it would be like if you asked me to come back. For a brief moment, I'm alive again.

Although I've distanced myself from you, I pray that you'll come around. I just hope you miss me and things fall into place.

I love you.

I want to come home so badly.

Female/26

COMMENTS:

>> Sometimes when you are heart broken, it is easy to get caught up in concentrating on the dream of what you had, or could have, and not concentrate on the reality. The reality is that if he wanted you

that much, and believed in you that much, he would ask you back and give you the choice. It's hard to take, but blaming yourself is putting off facing up to the reality that you need to get over this guy. It is putting off making the choice to heal. It happened the way it was supposed to happen. Now is your time to carve out a new path instead of holding on to the dream that you had/have. Don't cry because it is over, smile because it happened. It taught you lessons, you shouldn't lose them. It is up to you to choose to move on from this. I don't mean that to sound like it is easy, it's not ¬— but it is possible.

SECRET REGRET: I regret that you are a dork,

And I am a dork,

And we are perfect for one another,

And you know it.

I regret that I thought that you knew it. I regret that I couldn't just keep my mouth shut. I regret that if you confess you have feelings for someone, and they say nothing back, it means the feeling isn't mutual. I regret realizing I'm not good enough for you only after I convinced myself that you are the only one for me.

SECRET REGRET: I regret bullying you in the past. I remember you coming to my aid when I had no one else. I regret the day I became popular and you remained a loser. I constantly made fun you. I am really sorry. You were one of the best people I had ever met. I'm sorry for being so horrible. 15F

COMMENTS:

>> I didn't "remain a loser" and the fact that you say that proves you have so much more growing to do.

SECRET REGRET: Honestly when I look back on my short life so far, I realize that some pretty not-so-wonderful things have happened to me. I held on to regrets a bit longer than I would have liked to. I stayed with an ex who made me feel like everything I did was wrong. I didn't trust my instincts the first time I ended the relationship. I kept trying to please everyone and get my 'daddy' back. I was jealous of my stepmom and siblings for taking my 'daddy' away from me, and then I learned to turn my jealously into anger toward my father. I have also learned that everything not-so-wonderful that has happened to me in the past led me to be the person I am today. Today I love the life I live and I don't live it for anyone else's approval. I live for me and my personal happiness and I have come to terms with the fact that what I do might not appease everyone. I am in an amazing relationship with the man of my dreams and like I have always wanted since I can remember starting to like boys.

So "God Bless the broken road." Live your life to the fullest and try to go through it without regrets.

SECRET REGRET: If I had a second chance, I'd have not been so stubborn with my friend who is now dead. I was always the one to call and keep in touch. So after my last visit to her home, I decided to hell with her, I'm not calling her until she calls me. The only call I got was about a year later, when her husband called me to tell me she died ... at age 49. I wish I still had her in my life ... despite the fact that her alcoholism made her a lot of work. She was one of the most interesting people I've known. I miss her.

SECRET REGRET: I regret everyday that no one knows that he is your son. I regret that another man is raising him as his own and that one day the truth could come out and destroy our family and your heart. I regret not giving you the chance to be a father, no person deserves the pain or heartache that this situation could cause.

SECRET REGRET: I regret that we had that stupid fight and that we were both too stubborn to back down. I regret the fact that you're gone now and I'll never get the chance to tell you I'm sorry, and that I want us to work it out. But most of all I regret the fact that because of all of this I'm scared to come to your funeral because I'm not sure if you would have wanted me there. It kills me that you died alone thinking I hated you when really I was just hurt and saddened by what happened. I wish I would have picked up the phone and fixed things instead of writing this regret :(

I'm sorry x

COMMENTS:

>> I think if he were to know that you feel so horrible about the whole situation, he wouldn't be happy that you feel so bad. Live on happy in the memory of him. He probably would've wanted that. And as for you not letting him know how you feel. I'm sure he knows ... wherever he is ...

SECRET REGRET: If I had a second chance to do ONE thing differently in my life, I would not have raised my fist back at you.

I might have stopped to think about why you were raising yours in the first place. I might've noticed that the reason you felt you needed to break me was because you, too, were broken inside. You felt like you needed someone to hurt – the way you did – so you wouldn't feel alone, so someone would finally understand. I could have realized that the difference between us is that you are too afraid or prideful to admit your heart is in pieces. I would have let you know that it's okay to not know how to put yourself back together ... that you're not alone in your struggles. That we can do this together.

Violence was not the answer, we both know that. Neither of us will ever get a second chance to rewind and take back those physical and mental fights, but I want you to know that we can both take a deep breath and look forward. It doesn't have to happen again. I think I might have told you that, more than anything, I'm here for you. Daughters rely on their mothers ... but sometimes, it's okay for the mother to rely on her daughter.

Female, 18

SECRET REGRET: I wouldn't have gotten so mad over the little things. I would appreciate the good things. I would smile more and complain less because I was loved.

SECRET REGRET: If I could change one thing, it would be that I would have "come out" to my parents when I was a teenager. I was afraid they would stop loving me, and I never told them. Now my father is dead. He would've helped so much – and my mother will never understand. I feel isolated from my family, and always will. I wish I had just worked up the courage to tell them who I really am. I wish I could have had the courage to trust their love, or at least to let them realize that I am one of "those" people my mom hates so much. I'm someone they can be proud of, but it's too late to try to make them understand now.

Female, 45

COMMENTS:

>> I waited to come out and my father was dead already but I think he knew ... and I thought the same about my mother, but her love for me overcame all that, and she accepted me for who I am, and for once, I felt free of fear. I hope the same for you.

SECRET REGRET: I regret the limits of my upbringing. I regret that my ancestors have determined what I must do even though I really don't want to. I regret that, for the first time in my life, I found someone who I could see myself being with but I just cannot. I regret that there is such a thing as different skin colours! I regret that you will never know how I feel because even thinking it is a sin in my world. I regret that I have to look at you everyday knowing that I have to keep my mouth shut or risk being disowned. And most of all, I regret that just typing these words strikes fear into my heart.

COMMENTS:

>> My long-time boyfriend broke up with me because of his family. They told him they would disown him if he chose a life with me ... because I am not Jewish. They acknowledged that when he was with

www.SecretRegrets.com

me he was the happiest they had ever seen him, but I'm not Jewish so I wasn't good enough. I hate how close-minded they are and how close-minded it has forced him to be.

>> The man of my dreams is a secret to my family because he's white and my Asian parents would not allow it. I feel guilt everyday because his family has welcomed me with open arms. Hang in there.

>> I come from an Arab background and understand completely how you feel. I wish it were as simple for me as just being disowned. If I disgrace my family, it means my father can come after me and kill me. My mother is American and is afraid he would kill her too, yet it was okay for them to marry and be happy. I don't understand a relationship when you're afraid he will shoot you for dishonoring his family, yet still they love each other. I hate my culture, and heritage. It isn't as easy sometimes to just put your foot down. Sometimes you worry about your life and others' lives as well, yet every day I wonder why I have to protect my sister and my mother when they won't help me out. I understand where you are coming from and I'm sorry. No one should have to go through this.

>> Love is a good enough reason. Risk being disowned.

SECRET REGRET: I regret never telling anyone about the molestation. I know I was a kid, a scared and confused kid – but telling someone, ANYONE, instead of just pretending it didn't happen, would have saved me a lot of heartache. Trying to heal 12 years after the fact is ridiculously difficult. I regret all the time I've lost.

Female, 18

COMMENTS:

>> I didn't tell anyone about mine either. In fact I shoved it away. So far away that it regressed and came shooting back to me one night during a week long volunteer youth project when I was 700 miles from home. I have been dealing with it ever since. That was 15 years ago and it's difficult to get past. It affected me in ways I never would have imagined. I never thought I would be loved or be able to be touched in a way that didn't make me feel dirty or used. Today I'm married and have a child. I'm loved and can allow myself to be. It wasn't easy but it is possible. Life does get better and you're on the right path. Good luck to you.

SECRET REGRET: If I had a second chance to do ONE thing differently in my life, I would have let go of the idea of having a real father in my life. I would have stopped asking and seeking his attention and love. I would have stopped looking for him to save me from the life I had. I would have realized that he had a new life with his other children and new girlfriend. I would have let go, moved on and been happy. I would have realized that there was nothing wrong with me. IT WAS ALL HIM.

Male, 24

COMMENTS:

>> I'm so inspired by your post. The exact same thing happened to me. I was daddy's little girl until I was 13, when he met my step-mom. I was kicked out of the house and out of his life. Until this day, we really don't speak. I still seek attention from men because I lost the best man I had in my life. Hopefully things will get better for you and me. But it still pains me to think that I won't have my father to walk me down the aisle.

SECRET REGRET: I never would've become friends with them. They ruined who I used to be.

SECRET REGRET: At this moment I am fearful. I regret what is yet to come. I met you 7 months ago. You've made me feel loved, happy, and confident. No one else has ever done that for me in the same way. But I tell you I love you when I'm not sure I really mean it. I regret we didn't meet years earlier, before I got screwed over by so many others. I've put up my defenses. I'm still hung up on feelings for the last guy who didn't appreciate me. I regret that my heart refuses to want you like I wish it would. You're so kind, honest and perfect for me. Your smile, your hugs ... sometimes I never want to let go. But for some reason I'm still not satisfied. In truth, you're not quite attractive or smart enough to be the man I imagine I'll marry. I regret that I am selfishly clinging on to the love you give me because I'm too scared to be alone again. Perhaps forever. I'm too frightened to lose you and take a gamble on the future.

I love you but I'm not in love with you. You've quickly become one of my best friends, but I just can't see us lasting forever. My biggest regret will be having to say goodbye to you one day. To leave you hurt and confused, wondering what has changed. Nothing. I'll just finally be telling the truth rather than falsely declaring love for you. I regret typing this message, as I can't deny the truth now it's set down in black and white. I hope I have the courage to break it off soon before you waste any more time on me. You deserve so much more than this. I do love you. I hope I change my mind so this regret won't ever come true.

COMMENTS:

>> I know exactly what you are going through. I broke off the relationship for his good, so think about him and do the right thing. It will probably hurt but be proud of your decision. Take some time off and work on your wounded heart. All the best.

>> Fifteen years later, and an ill child who needs two parents to care for her, I realize that my husband felt about me exactly the way you feel about this guy. He actually told me once, after we were married, that while we were dating he didn't think I was pretty enough to marry. Just leave him, and save him, and you, all the suffering and guilt. You know what? After all these years, he probably loves me more than I do him. So in the end, you might find yourself more hurt than you now think he will be. I wish my husband had not "settled" with me. It would have hurt then, but I could have found someone who loved me as much as I love him.

SECRET REGRET: I would have not pulled that trigger.

SECRET REGRET: I regret ducking in the back seat of your mom's car during our freshman year carpool. I was embarrassed by the car. I was stupid, shallow, young, and didn't realize it at the time, but I was the only embarrassing part of that equation. I know you know I did that. I'm so sorry. It haunts me to this day.

SECRET REGRET: I regret that we have drifted apart. You are my very best friend, and I love you more than you will ever know. I regret not having the courage to tell you how much it hurts me that you always choose your boyfriend over me. That somehow, our friendship no longer matters to you as much as it used to.

We have known each other since we were 6 years old. We experienced our first love, our first loss together. And unfailingly we were always there for each other no matter what. We would laugh until we cried, and my favorite memory was when we danced around to Disney songs in your living room at 6 in the morning after coming home from a party. I don't know anybody who was as close as us.

We used to sit in your window, eating your mom's homemade buns, and talk about everything we dreamed of becoming. We were supposed to travel through Europe together, move in together and have the time of our lives. We planned to grow old together and have wheelchair races in the nursing home, when we could no longer walk.

When we both started having serious relationships this changed. You lose yourself in your relationship, and all of a sudden I no longer matter. I regret having all kinds of faith in you and our friendship, and constantly being disappointed by you. I regret knowing that I will drop everything and come running if you want me to, but you will no longer return the favour.

I sincerely regret knowing that I will always miss you desperately, but you no longer care as much. I regret having to let you go, and I can only hope that one day you will realize that losing your best friend of 17 years is not worth whatever you feel you're gaining from clinging to your boyfriend and ignoring everyone else.

I hope you don't end up alone. I love you.

Female, 23

COMMENTS:

>> That actually happened to me. And I let her do it. I let her be her own person. Once that relationship ended and she saw the real world again, she saw I was going through a tough time, and she called me. I never thought we would be close again but I was wrong. She just needed to see everything else again. And some people's personality is that clingy-kind-of-need-only-them kind of

thing, which sadly means you need to find a new friend to add to your collection until she wants to come back. I have some good friends because of that, too. Good luck, I'm sorry you have to go through this like I did.

>> I've been in this situation before, but I was the girl who wasn't being a good friend. Don't let her go. I have to say that the reason (although I do take full blame for pushing my friend aside like I did) this happened to me was because I was in an abusive relationship. I didn't know how to get out and I was stuck. I still talked to my friend and was there for her,, but not like I had been before. He finally broke up with me and I went back to who I had been before. I was happier, but it took him breaking up with me to realize what I had been missing. Don't be a bad friend. Your friend still needs you.

>> I feel like this was either written to me or about me, that's how close my situation was to yours. I wish things could be different, as I was the one who distanced myself from her. But it's so hard when you find the man that you love and want to spend your life with and she can't accept it. I never in my life wanted to choose between my best friend and my boyfriend. She forced that choice on me. Our being best friends meant that I either chose her or him. I choose him, whom I'm still with 2 years later. It sucks, and it's hard to no longer have that rock sometimes. But I know that I'm a better person without her.

SECRET REGRET: I regret that I was the other woman. I opened up a Pandora's box of pain for her and for me. I won him and then he proceeded to cheat on me. He even cheated on me with her, the woman I stole him from. He hurt me in so many ways, physically, mentally, and emotionally. I stayed for so long. Break ups and getting back together, when I knew I should stay away. I kept doing this until I finally didn't. I finally met someone else who allowed me to be myself and who loves me. The silver lining, in apologizing to her, the one I stole him from, is that we started to talk. We even became friends. We also both realized exactly how long you really did play us both. I regret giving you that control over me. I regret letting you hurt me. I regret hurting another woman. I regret devaluing myself.

COMMENTS:

>> That's why I'm gonna end everything tomorrow.

SECRET REGRET: If I had a second chance to do ONE thing differently in my life, I would have never let you abuse me as long as you did. I would have walked away. I would have broken up with you the first time you hit me. I would have ended it the first time you told me I was worthless and weak. I would have told your girlfriend the truth, because now I have found a wonderful man who truly loves, cares and adores me, and every time he lifts his hand to my face to kiss me, or grabs my arm suddenly to spin me around, I recoil as if he's going to hurt me. He never would and he never will, but you did. And now I'm not sure how long it will take before that instinct you unfortunately drilled into me will go away. I hate you for it, and I hate myself for letting it happen.

COMMENTS:

>> I've been where you are. Learn to forgive him and you will learn to forgive yourself and you will be on the road of healing.

SECRET REGRET: I regret that for the past 6+ months I have been wallowing in what I did wrong and spending so much time thinking about it and going over it again and again. Last night I told myself, for the millionth time, "Just Forgive Yourself!" And I think I've started to. I have been telling myself this for so long but I never thought it would happen. It feels great to have a little hope again!

COMMENTS:

>> What you have written is something my best friend has been asking me to do time and time again for the past year ... yet for the first time ever, I have really heard it and I have promised myself that I will do everything in my power to do it ... to forgive myself. And find my way back to being the person I was before the illness engulfed and suffocated me. Thank you!

SECRET REGRET: If I had a second chance to do ONE thing differently in my life, I would have taken you back when you wanted me ... because now, I am alone. And you are happy without me, and after being with you for four years, I never realized how much you truly loved me. Instead, I let you beg for me to take you back ... and when I FINALLY came to my senses, it was too late.

Here I am left in the dust, begging you to take me back. Talk about role reversal ... talk about how pathetic I am.

Female, 21

SECRET REGRET: I would have given love a chance.

SECRET REGRET: I will forever regret saying goodnight early that January night, 26 years ago, because right after I left, you were killed in an accident. We were both kids hanging out in Times Square at Playland playing video games and somebody tried (unsuccessfully) to pick my pocket. I got nervous after that, and wanted to leave. I didn't tell you why. You walked me to the train with our friend, and I got on and you stayed. I will forever regret leaving early that night because you might still be here if I had stayed. We were cousins but you were my brother and I miss you. That is my biggest regret.

SECRET REGRET: I regret not leaving you when I first found out you didn't love me.

Now it's many heartbreaking years later and we have children.

Now I feel I am stuck.

I regret not getting an education, so that I could support myself and our children without your money.

I regret that I have fallen in love with a man that I can't possibly be with.
You see, he deserves to build a family. Have his own children. Now that I can no longer have children, I can't ask him to give that up for me.

My children and I come as a team, and while he WOULD love them and treat them as his own, I don't want to stumble across his post on this page one day – regretting giving up his chance at a family for me.

I regret the years I gave you.
I regret the tears I cried for you.
I regret the pain I felt for you.
I regret the life I led for you.

I regret ... YOU.

Female/31

COMMENTS:

>> Awww. He can still accept your children as his own, and that can be his family. It could work. It's happened. Or you can adopt.

SECRET REGRET: If I had a 2nd chance at life, I wouldn't be gay, because I secretly think it's a sin and it's just too much to deal with sometimes. I want the pain to go away.

COMMENTS:

>> Don't EVER be ashamed of who you are!

>> You can't help who you are attracted to, and this does not define who you are. Stand tall, be proud.

SECRET REGRET: I regret the silence. Ten years ago, we were both in fifth grade, you were the new kid in class. You raised your hand a lot, you were kind of nerdy, but hey, so was I.

Then in the hallway, a few days after your first day, two boys shoved you against the locker and called you a nigger.

I regret that I did nothing. That I shrank against the walls, something I do best. I'd never heard that word in person, meant as an act of hate. I have nightmares about it. Reoccurring nightmares. To know that all I had to do was tell a teacher, or tell those guys back off, or to just ask if you were ok. I did nothing.

I regret the silence.

22/Female

COMMENTS:

>> You were wrong, but you were young. Time to forgive yourself.

>> So many children are put in this situation, and few stand up. You were young, and far from being the only one who stayed silent. It is so important that you forgive yourself.

>> Wow, this one really touched me. Thank you for sharing. It's beautifully written. I hope that reading this will give me the great courage to stand up against the bullies if I ever find myself in a similar situation.

SECRET REGRET: I regret the small-minded people I'm faced with every day at work. I regret that I let their bitchy, two-faced rants behind closed doors to constantly boil up inside me but never get out. I regret that she will always think she's getting away with it, she'll always think that she's playing the game, on everybody's side when really everyone feels sorry for her. I regret that my last day is a long time from now. But trust me, when it is, I will tell every single idiot how I really feel, and destroy their image of me being sweet, nice and reliable. I'll be sure to shock them all.

In an unhappy job/20

COMMENTS:

>> I can tell you right now that in 10, 20, or 30 years from now, no matter what job you hold, it will always be like this. Ignore them the best you can, do your job well, and at the end of the day, surround yourself with people who love you and care about you.

>> Some words of wisdom: if and when you quit this job, do it with grace and class. Don't tell everybody where to go and how to get there. In the end, you are the one who looks foolish. Also you

never know when you may run into your former co-workers. Don't burn your bridges. Cattiness is in every workplace, not just yours. It will eat you up inside if you let all the drama get to you. Trust me, I know how you feel but it's always better to take the high road.

SECRET REGRET: I regret a lot of things ... but mainly I regret my reaction to my Dad's terminal illness. I don't know whether mine was a normal reaction, but I wish that, upon hearing that he will not be around to see me through university, or to meet his grandchildren – I had thought about him. Instead, like the child I seem to be, I went into self-destruct mode ... thinking of no one but myself. I very quickly turned into a monster, destroying the relationship I used to have with him.

Now, I think back to before I knew, and I wish it could be like that again. But I know it can't because of all the awful things I have said.

I regret ruining the last chance I had with him.

So I'm sorry Daddy, I never meant any of it. I was just scared of the inevitable, of losing you. And now I miss you, and I love you.

Female, 16.

COMMENTS:

>> I really know what you've been through. My mom passed away. She had terminal cancer. In her last days, she was like screaming out of pain, I was a very good supportive daughter throughout her illness. But in those few last days, I couldn't bear the screaming and seeing her in agony. I was so mad at her and I kept saying in my mind, "Oh God! I can't hear the screaming anymore!" and I used to go out for a walk or even go shopping, as if nothing matters, and I'm that strong evil person who does not give a damn. When she passed away, I knew that I was in so much pain for her, so I just needed to be mad at someone. I love her to death. She's the best mom, and best person ever!

>> Oh, you poor girl. With tears in my eyes as I write this ... I was 35 when my dad was diagnosed with cancer and died, and I didn't know how to handle it either. Of course you fell apart. He was wiser than you know right now, but someday you'll understand. He knew you were just a child and he

forgives you. Wait till you have children of your own. Even when they're downright evil, you still love them. There is simply NOTHING my kids could do that would make me stop loving them. I can tell by your emotional maturity and deep regret that you must have had good parents. Give your mom a chance. Let her know how you feel. Show her your posted regret. Trust can be re-earned. Forgive yourself and live the most wonderful life you know how to from here on. Honor him by being your best you.

SECRET REGRET: I regret not caring about my weight until it's almost too late. At close to 400 lbs, I am facing certain death, but because I have to taste a little of my addiction every day, it's impossible for me to quit completely because I need to live. I regret not speaking up and telling someone I need help ... I still do.

26/F

SECRET REGRET: I regret the fact that you love her. That I have to sit alone at night and wonder if we weren't having this baby together, you'd still do all of the things you do for me just because you love me.

I regret the fact that a baby had to change you. That I couldn't.

That maybe this baby was a weapon for me to use against you. I regret that even knowing about your past, I still got involved with you. And now I have to wonder every day if you mean it when you say, "I love you."

I regret not knowing if I really do love you, or if I was just so desperate to hear it from someone that I would say it to you just to hear it back. I regret that I hurt him and left him to be with you.

Now I'm 19 and pregnant with your child wondering how long it will last.

COMMENTS:

>> Children change you. Even if you split, the baby will help you grow into a different person; one who prioritizes life completely differently. Don't let him walk all over you. Don't use the baby as a tool against him, and don't let him use it against you. And that guy you hurt? Maybe he can find it in his heart to forgive you, and help you raise the baby. Life twists in unexpected ways, and nothing is definite

SECRET REGRET: I regret using shopping as a way of dealing with my unhappiness in the past. Now I'm truly happy in my life situation, but my past mistakes are still being paid for, literally. I regret that I will still be paying for my past unhappiness for many years to come and that I feel like I'm completely drowning in debt.

33/F

COMMENTS:

>> I have done the exact same thing. Same age, same gender. The weight and guilt is incredible but I try to focus on how good it feels when I make my monthly payment. All that crap I bought didn't make me any happier. You're not alone.

>> But you won't regret the lesson. Clear those debts and your soul will be free forever. Don't be afraid to contact a professional to help you with a payment plan.

SECRET REGRET: I regret choosing him, because he looked good on paper, when I was so, so in love with you. You and I were best friends who happened to fall in love. When you would touch me, it sent chills down my spine. I never felt that with him.

It's been three years, and you still are not going out with anyone, but I married the guy that looked good on paper – the guy who cheated on me, lied to me, and is now divorcing me. I regret that right now, I could be in your arms and in your love, but am not because I chose a different path. I regret that I could not stop loving you, and that you still haunt me every day. If only you would still love me after what I did ... if only you could forgive me ...

F/24

COMMENTS:

>> Sounds to me like you need to tell him how you feel. Maybe it will work out, maybe it won't ... but at least you can say you tried ... one last apology. Perhaps one way or the other it will help you move on with your life. You only get the one, after all. My hopes are with you. Be strong!!

>> I know I'd take you back if I were him. Just tell him how you feel. Life has given you this. Take your second chance and go. If your marriage is lost and you feel for this man as much as you do, you would be a fool not to admit to him how wrong you were.

SECRET REGRET: If I had a second chance to do ONE thing differently in my life, I would have chosen to be with you when you asked me to. I couldn't do it because I was too afraid of what my friends would think. And now, years later, none of them are even in my life anymore, but I still talk to and see you every day. Now that it's way too late to do anything about it, I am desperately jealous of your girlfriend and I can't get over what I almost, but never, had.

Female, 22

SECRET REGRET: I regret staying in the car while my favorite cat was put down. I know he was in pain. I know he must have been so scared. He was the only friend I had for so long. The bond between people and their pets is amazing. I regret not being strong enough :(

F/17

COMMENTS:

>> I work in an animal hospital. We euthanize animals often and you can rest assured that your pet was in loving arms when he/she took their last breath. We hold them, stroke them, talk to them ... all while it is taking place. They know you love them and maybe just couldn't bring yourself to be there. Hold their memories in your heart and let go of the guilt you feel. They wouldn't want you to feel that. Just remember their unconditional love and give that back out into the world.

>> Having my dog put down in my arms was the most horrific moment of my life. It's a double-edged sword. I was happy I was there for her but seeing her look up at me while she died is something I'll never forget. Holding her back when she tried to nip at the nurse when she put the needle in broke my heart. And lifting her head off of my lap to get her collar off once she was gone was traumatic. I went into the parking lot to drive away and threw up. I understand and I'm sorry.

SECRET REGRET: If I could change one thing, I never would have met you. I swear, there are very few things I wouldn't give to just take back every moment and effort I wasted on you. I wish it was easier to let go ... people tell me to just walk away and wash my hands and my mind of you ... but I'm not that tough.

People tell me I'm better than you (those select few who know about "us," do, anyway) and I want so badly to act on that. I never want to see you, be around you or even hear about you, ever again.

For the past 4 years, you have done nothing but ruin me ... and I allow you to do it. Over and over again. You have a hold on me like no person or thing ever has. I hate how I know in my otherwise brilliant mind that you are awful ... horrible ... destructive.

But I can't seem to ever shake you, for good. As many times as I've tried and successfully walked away for awhile, it never lasts. My efforts against you are useless. You're killing me. I hate you, cocaine.

Female, 23

COMMENTS:

>> Stay strong. I just went through this with my husband. You must surround yourself with people who will support you! You must leave all your friends that you think are your friends behind. They are not your friends as much as you would like to think they are. It is a very hard thing to quit because I see my husband struggle with it everyday. It is a lifelong struggle. Just make sure to go to support meetings and make sure to get a sponsor when you go. They will help you when you are feeling the urge. I will pray for you, and I know you can do it. Good luck and stay strong!

>> Listen to "The Girl you Lost to Cocaine" by Sia. It helps you look at your addiction as if you were your clean friend. LFT.

>> (Update from original poster, 2 days later) I'd like to thank those of you who left comments of encouragement. I am the girl who wrote this post and I've not touched cocaine since I wrote it. It's going to be quite a journey, but I thank each of you for helping me to kick it off. To "Anonymous" ... tell your husband I wish him the best of luck and all the success in the world. And LFT ... THANK YOU for that song.

SECRET REGRET: I regret having posted a regret here. F/18

COMMENTS:

>> Me too. I thought it would be good for me to actually get something off my chest and into the written word. Maybe the person that my secret was about would read it and immediately know, and try to undo the regret. But nothing magical came from me posting my secret regret. So I guess it's not in posting my regret, I regret getting my hopes up that something would come from my post.

>> You post for yourself, not for the person who caused the regret. The same way, you forgive for yourself, not for the other person. When we forgive, it doesn't mean we agree with what the person did or said, but it's to free ourselves so we can move on with our lives. My heart goes out to you who have posted here and now regret it. I hope that you'll let go of the real issue and move on with your lives.

>> Don't regret writing something on here, because I'm sure it has helped or influenced someone somehow, and without reading your regret they might not have made the decision they did.

SECRET REGRET: If I had a second chance to do one thing in my life differently, I would not have taunted my sister for being fat when we were children. Now I'm the fat one and she's the skinny one. Deep down, I think this is God's way of punishing me.

Age 26, Female

SECRET REGRET: I regret nothing yet I regret everything. I regret everything I have ever done with you. I regret the day I met you. The day I fell in love with you. The days I sat there listening to you go on about the girls you like, the days you went on about your life. I regret letting you become my best friend. I regret not taking my chance and changing the relationship we have. I regret being scared of telling you everything. Yet I know you will understand. I want to just walk up to you one day, and kiss you. Not one of those baby pecks on the lips, I want the Noah and Ali kiss in the rain during the Notebook. You're the best thing that ever happened to me. When I'm with you, I'm so comfortable, you're my everything, yet I'm your nothing. I regret letting myself fall for you so hard. I have crashed and burned to the ground now, and I'm totally broken up about you. You were the one to keep me going at my weakest point yet you were the one who brought me there. I regret not leaving you when I had the chance; I regret not wanting to move on from you.

I don't regret our friendship.

I just regret it not becoming more than just that.

SECRET REGRET: If I had a second chance, I would not have shot you. I was angry and not thinking rationally, but that is no excuse. I have spent all the years since regretting my actions. I am sorry and I will always love you.

43/M

SECRET REGRET: If I could change one thing, I would go back and never, ever let them pull the plug on you. I've done research, and doctors say that chances of waking up from a coma only start to go down after a month or two. You were only in the hospital for a week. I know I was only thirteen, but I was your only daughter, and if I had said no I'm sure they wouldn't have done it. I miss you so much, Mom. Every day. I'll regret what I did to you until the day I die.

Female, 19

COMMENTS:

>> Your mother's death is not your fault. I'm sure you were advised by her doctors that this was in her best interest. You did the right thing, and you can rest assured that your mother is proud of you. Now, live your life in a way that honors your mother. God bless you.

SECRET REGRET: If I had a second chance to do one thing differently in my life, I would have been honest with my ex when he asked if I'd met someone else. Because I had, and I wanted you the minute I laid eyes on you, so there was no point in denying it really. As it was, he believed we still had a chance and now he won't speak to me ...

And the worst part is ... if I had to choose one of you to have in my life ... it would still be him.

Female Age: 22

COMMENTS:

>> Well. That hit close to home.

SECRET REGRET: I used to think that my biggest regret was being born. So many days go by and I just want to end my existence. But I think that may just be my problem, I exist. I don't live. And that is my biggest regret.

COMMENTS:

>> I feel the exact same way. Thank you for putting it into words to remind me. I need to do something soon. I need to live.

>> The choice between living and merely existing is yours to make. It is also a choice that is never to late to make. Choose to do more. Choose to live.

SECRET REGRET: If I had a second chance to do ONE thing differently in my life, I would never let you convince me that our friendship would never transfer into a lasting romantic relationship, that we would never work. Because 10 years and two marriages later I still long to hear your voice in my ear, have your hands touch my skin, and be fully enveloped in your love. I never expected to want you, to need you, to miss you as I have all these years. You are my best friend but you should be my husband. You are my confidant but you should be my lover. You are a hundreds of amazing memories but you should be the father of my two children. I will love like no other and be with you when ever I have the chance. You will always be my destiny and is sucks we are both married to other people. 38/F

SECRET REGRET: I wish I had never been unfaithful. No one deserves it less than you do. I feel sorrow every day since then, and know I have sinned against you and our family. I pray for forgiveness every day but I will never tell you about what I did. You being hurt to the core by my actions will never help anyone.

SECRET REGRET: I regret ever coming to this school. All it has caused me is pain and torment. I've met some of the worst people that I will ever meet in my life. The people at this place have made my life a living hell. They've destroyed my self-esteem and warped my view of humankind. I'm so glad that I'm leaving this "Christian" school for a public school next year. Maybe there I'll meet someone who won't ruin my life.

14/F

COMMENTS:

>> Have you considered that maybe it isn't the Christianity of the school, but the age? Fourteen is when you really start to see how ugly humankind can be ... I wouldn't want you to give up on an entire religion for a bad experience.

SECRET REGRET: If I had a second chance, I would have never, EVER looked at pornography. I want to make the images go away. It demeans women, and destroys men.

34/M

SECRET REGRET: If I could change one thing, I would never have secretly resented you for all the time I had to spend with you in the summer. I used to be so angry when I had to go there and spend my days at your house because you were stuck in a wheelchair and needed someone with you at all times. If I could change it, I would make sure that I cherished every moment I spent with you because after you died, all I was left with was sadness and regret. All the times we did share together are tainted in my mind because of how ashamed of myself I am.

25/F

SECRET REGRET: I regret not having it out with you. I wish I would have thrown a fit years ago instead of putting up with her abuse just so that I could have a relationship with you. I wish I would have stood up for myself and told you that I needed my Dad to stick up for me, even if it was your girlfriend I needed you to stand up to. I wish I would have gone head-to-head with her years ago, shown her for what she is. Instead, I kept trying to make friends with her to make it stop. I kept looking the other way while she smeared me to you and the rest of our family. I let everyone believe her lies because I didn't want to fight, I wanted you to see it on your own and stick up for me.

Instead, you died believing her lies and garbage about me. I'll always regret not setting things straight. I never expected to lose you so soon and I definitely never thought you'd die without seeing me for who I really am. I wish you could have seen clearly that I'm not a monster. The monster was sharing your home with you. It hasn't been a month since you've died and she's clearing you out of your home, she destroyed the file that had your last wishes spelled out, and is taking everything you worked for. I won't fight her for your estate. You wanted it in thirds, but it's all going to her. Do you see the truth now from wherever you are? I won't fight her for your money.

I'm content with the knowledge that she's out of my life and my children's lives for good. All I wanted of yours was your dictionary. I asked and she said no. I got it for me though, and every time I need to look something up for school, I'll look it up in that big blue book that you always pointed me towards. It's my way of having you with me while I continue working to obtain a college education and while I continue to work to support myself and your grandchildren alone, as a single mom. I hope that wherever you are, you see things clearly. I regret that you never saw that I wasn't a bad daughter, or a bad mother. I regret that I ever let her into my life, to try to keep you in it. I should have called her out for what she is. While your EX wife stayed at the cemetery when they lowered your casket, so that you wouldn't be buried alone, your "lifetime companion" went straight to the work of cleaning you out of your home, your car. She went directly to work at destroying your last wishes that were written down and trying to take your entire estate. I regret that you're not here now to tell me what you want me to do now that you are able to see truth. I'll tell you that I'm not going to fight it. I'll let her take your entire estate, because the money doesn't matter to me.

My plan is the same as it was before you died. Take care of my babies, work, and finish school. I'll do it on my own, just like I have been for the last year. My success will be my own. She will get nothing from me in her old age, no care, nothing. I hope that she saves enough of your money to take care of herself, because your final gift to me is freedom from the monster that you brought into my life.

Maybe I'll regret that someday, but I doubt it.

COMMENTS:

>> Your dad knows everything and, if he could, he'd tell you that he is incredibly proud of you. She'll get hers one day ... hope the money keeps her warm at night.

SECRET REGRET: I regret waking up that morning when I was 7 and hearing my dad come home from a fishing trip to find you, my mother, in bed with the man you are now married to. I regret that I let your mistakes make me so unhappy, to the point that I wanted to commit suicide. I regret the pain and hurt I had to watch my father go through when you left him for that man.

I regret growing up, without a mother, because you left to go overseas with him.

I regret making the same mistakes that you made, and not learning from them and now feeling like I am totally untrustworthy and incapable of loving someone. I don't even know who I am. My whole world is a complete lie. Nobody knows me, and I'm scared that if they did, nobody would ever love me again. I regret that I can't stop making these mistakes.

I feel so alone. I regret I am exactly like you, yet I still give you grief over what you did.

F/26

SECRET REGRET: I regret trying to be with you even after I knew you didn't want me anymore. I knew from the beginning that "friends with benefits" always leaves one person hurt, but I never expected that for the first time, it would be me. I regret that in college, I became someone I never wanted to be. I'm only glad that having you break my heart helped me to see it.

F/18

SECRET REGRET: If I could do it over, I would spend more time with my mother in the last five years of her life. I thought there was more time. I was very busy with my own life, and I was secretly angry with her for being so demanding. I'd been taking care of her since 1981 and she seemed unwilling to do anything – in my opinion – to relieve her own boredom and depression. I took good care of her, but what she really wanted was for me to just hang out with her – playing Scrabble and watching Animal Planet on TV. It made me irritable because I had so little free time and that was not how I felt I should be spending it. Then she just died in her sleep 3 years ago with no warning. Now I'd give anything to play Scrabble with her one more time, even though she ALWAYS beat me.

61/F

COMMENTS:

>> Thank you for posting this<3. It makes me realize that I shouldn't take my mom for granted. I know that your mom is looking down from heaven and loves you. Nothing compares to a mother's love.

>> I completely understand your statement. My mother passed away 6/7/08 very unexpectedly. I would give anything just to see her name on my caller ID ... I think of all those times that I saw her calling and said, "I don't have time for this," ... now all I have is time to think and regret about all those moments forever lost.

SECRET REGRET: My biggest regret is spending 11 years missing you. You chose to leave us. I was only in 3rd grade. How can you leave your grandchildren? How can you disown your son? I never understood you, but for 11 years I've held a grudge, wasted my energy on missing you. I've finally seen what real grandparents are like and I've come to figure out you don't deserve my anger or my love.

F/19

SECRET REGRET: I regret forgetting my phone. If I had just grabbed it before I left, you never would've found those text messages and it wouldn't have ended like this – you drunk and upset, your best friend with a head wound on your couch, and me a nervous wreck. If I just would've grabbed the phone before I left.

F/18

SECRET REGRET: If I could change the timing, I would in a heartbeat.

So much time had passed, so many years we worked side by side. We were such a great team. Eventually we just couldn't stand it any longer, we had to give in to the desire but the timing was all wrong, and so we were all wrong, despite the fact that if I had allowed myself to speak the truth to my heart, I would have cried out in earnest over how much I loved you. Every time we were together I couldn't believe how right, how good and how perfect you felt to me. I loved how you smiled at me, how you touched me and kissed me. Your lips were so soft and everything about you was willing. It was so evident in your eyes. You simply swept me away, but there was another man, another life and another heart waiting, and I had to choose what was best for me, and for my child. I knew it couldn't be you. There was too much history, too much unwritten. I couldn't have done what I did if I didn't love you, but between us we didn't have something that I knew would endure. And to this day, more than seven years later, I still am haunted and stuck with the memories.

The ache of that realization can still bring me to my knees.

Maybe I don't want to let go even though I know I have to. My husband doesn't know, and he never will. I love you and I miss you and I think of you daily. I wish I could tell you.

44/F

SECRET REGRET: I regret not speaking up when people say 'faggot' or 'bitch' or 'nigger' as insults. I regret not speaking up at every chance I get to stop oppression on a day-to-day level.

SECRET REGRET: If I could, I would change the fact that I left you that summer. I was younger, and more naive. I didn't realize just how much I actually loved you and how lucky I was that I had found you so early. But it was high school. It was summer. Everything was going to be new and exciting and I thought being with you would hold me back. It was fun for a while. We both found other people. I jumped from girl to girl and you found him. You lost your virginity to him, and then everything went wrong.

You split up the summer after your senior year, and I was the only one who was there for you. We hadn't spoken the entire year after our break up, but I never stopped loving you, no matter what girl I was with that week. I never did anything with them. I wanted you.

I wish I had told you then.

Because now that we're together again, I still can't get over the fact that he has a part of you that I can never get. And I hate him for it.

19/M

SECRET REGRET: I wish I had never hit him. It's my third charge. That first punch wasn't worth what it's brought me. Now I've f'd up my entire life. Saturday could be my last day of freedom all because I thought that I was some kind of badass.

Trust me, the jail time isn't worth it. Don't make the same mistake I did.

(Note: Saturday came and went, and the original poster did not return to post an update.)

SECRET REGRET: I regret looking in her diary. I knew I wouldn't like what I found, but now I know that my father had an affair and was with his mistress while I was being born. My mum thinks I hate him because I'm a typical teenager. I hate him because he's shallow and missed the birth of his only daughter. I regret looking at her e-mails to find that he never wanted me and tried to persuade her to get an abortion. Thanks Dad. Don't think you're getting an invite to my future.

Female, 19

COMMENTS:

>> Maybe his secret regret is everything that you just said. Just because you don't want something initially doesn't mean you don't love it after it happens. Just because he didn't want kids 19 years ago doesn't mean he doesn't love you now.

>> I don't think you're wrong to want him out of your life and your future, but hating him will only hurt you. There are people out there that choose to be heartless. Be a bigger person and have a better heart. Let go of the hate because it does nothing while inside of you.

SECRET REGRET: I'm going to make it so that I never have to say, "If I had a second chance" ... Before I leave, I'm going to tell you I'm still in love with you. Just you wait for it. 19/F

COMMENTS:

>> This post just seems too perfect to not be who I think it is. I'm not going to ask if it is you, but I really hope it is. If this is who I think it is then trust me ... I still love you too.

SECRET REGRET: I regret that I read all these regrets and hoped that I would see one from you. F/21

COMMENTS:

>> I do the same thing. You're not alone, I'm sure there are many out there who still hope, wish, pray with their hearts that one day, one will be about them, from that special someone. Of course there are others out there who have been disappointed and no longer believe. I hope I never lose faith in humanity. It's sites like this that keep it going some days.

SECRET REGRET: I regret that I will now sit here and read every single regret posted here, hoping that there is one from a certain person telling me that they regret breaking my heart and letting me go. And it breaks my heart more knowing I'll probably never see it.

F/20

COMMENTS:

>> You just wrote what I've been doing myself. I check the website daily, all the while knowing I'll never see the post I WANT to see. But I still come back anyway.

>> Miranda – I never wished to divorce you. I never stopped loving you, guess I never shall.

>> If only you were the 20/F I wrote about yesterday. But I know you aren't.

>> It has been almost two years and I still feel the same about him and I was searching for the post just like you were. You're not alone.

>> I've been in love with the same person for seven years. I come on here hoping for the same thing, or I read through all the posts that do say "I love you" and for a second I think it's for me, but then I'm back to real life and regretting every moment I spend without him.

>> (Update from the original poster): I am the author of this regret, and it makes me even more sad to know, that this regret was posted on my anniversary with my new boyfriend, that is 13 months. And yet my ex still haunts my mind.

SECRET REGRET: If I could change one thing I would have not said, "Please stay," when I really was hoping you'd leave and go back to Ontario. I love the kids I had with you, but I wish I had not endured everything else because I felt too sorry for you to make you go away.

SECRET REGRET: My biggest regret is agreeing to "friends with benefits." It eats me up inside to know that you want my body, but you don't actually care about me and what I have to say. I wish I could tell you that I want it all to be different, but I can't, because I would do anything to be with you, even under these circumstances. I regret that you don't love me, and that I lied to your face today when you asked me if I was agreeing – just to pretend like it could turn into something more. Yes. I will be pretending that, because it's the only way I'll be able to bear it.

SECRET REGRET: I regret that I've let my OCD completely control my life. I hate that I'm not strong enough to overcome it, and I'm too scared to ask for help. I regret that I can't explain it to the ones I love for fear of being laughed at or misunderstood.

COMMENTS:

>> Don't ever be afraid to ask for help. They may not understand right away but they won't laugh.

>> We already know, and none of us are laughing. We just accept it as part of the wonderfulness that is you.

>> You are not alone. There are so many of us out here, fearing the same thing. Finding someone to help you is the absolute hardest part right now, but waking up 5 years from now and realizing that you've missed out on your own life because of it would be even harder. There are some amazing people out there who have made it their life mission to help people like us, and they want to help. Good luck to you, you are never alone :)

SECRET REGRET: I wish I could erase the memory. I wish that I could erase the memory that you were in love with my best friend while you were going out with me. I knew long before you even told me. Now we are so in love and we've totally worked through all of that but it still kills me. It eats me up inside. I don't want that memory.

25/M

SECRET REGRET: I wouldn't have done all of the things I did with my best friend's ex.

SECRET REGRET: I regret not standing up to you sooner. You won't hurt her or me anymore. I still have lingering fears and nightmares, lingering memories that invade my relationship with my husband. It's something I'll have to work through so I don't make the same mistake she did, or worse, ruin a good relationship because of you.

I also regret not being able to express my fears and feelings about this with my husband. He is undoubtedly perfect for me and doesn't remind me of you. Still, thoughts of how you treated me, how you treated my mother, creep into my mind late at night as I lay next to my husband and I begin to worry and fear history repeating itself. I cry as quietly as I can until I fall asleep. Sometimes my husband wakes up before I fall asleep and notices. He holds me, trying to get me to tell him why I'm crying, before embracing me with such tenderness that I can't help but wonder at the differences among men and often cry harder.

My biggest non-regret is marrying him. Because I know I am safe, that I will never be tormented or dominated. I know love and compassion, and I won't live any longer without it.

19/F

COMMENTS:

>> Tell him, or else he'll always wonder if it's him, and that will be a weak spot in your marriage. A marriage needs communication to survive. He sounds like a good man. Do everything you can to hold on to your marriage with him. This requires trust, openness, honesty and knowing when to keep quiet and when not to.

>> You aren't the only one. Not by a long shot. And thank you for wording it so well.
I wish you the best in your marriage, and I hope that someday you feel ok telling your husband. I hope someday you don't have to cry yourself to sleep. I hope someday you heal, and that the scar isn't too big. *hugs*

SECRET REGRET: If I could change one thing in my life, it would be to have never let things end with my parents the way they did. I should have told you both about how I really felt about your problems, your getting a divorce, my mother finding a new man within a month of separation, her showering and being with him while me and my sister were in the next room weeks after.

I could have voiced my honest opinion. Maybe you would have thought about how it would affect us more. And even though I was only nine, I knew that sitting silently by and watching your marriage fall apart wasn't my fault, but I didn't plead for you to try counseling. And when Mom and her new boyfriend asked for our blessing for moving our family in with the other man, I said the opposite to what I felt. And even though he turned out to be a wonderful step-father (better than my own father was from then forth), I can't help, but wonder what if I said no it wasn't okay with me all those years ago.

Even if it did nothing, and things still ended up the same, I wouldn't feel like I couldn't have made it any easier for you to split up our family.

20/M

SECRET REGRET: I regret being married but having to have affairs with younger men in order to have sex at all. I love you, more than you could know, but the only thing saving our marriage is my straying from it.

COMMENTS:

>> It really amuses me to no end when people try to act like they're justified in cheating on their spouse. My favorite is when they actually go so far as to say that their cheating is "saving their marriage." Author, I don't know you or your husband personally, but I believe that your husband (like the rest of us) deserves a wife who is committed to him, and who, in times of struggle, won't act like they're a hero for screwing other men on the side.

SECRET REGRET: I regret never having the balls to tell you how I really felt about you. If I had of just told you. You would have told me you loved me too. But instead I had to find out from your best friend after your funeral. You were truly the most beautiful, amazing, smart person I have ever met. I miss you so much. The words I never said will haunt me until the day I die.

20/M

SECRET REGRET: I regret that some days I feel like I made a bad decision marrying an Army boy. I hate you being gone and hate that I thought I was strong enough to handle it. I love you with all of my heart and it is so unfortunate that the Army is the only reason we even got together in the first place. I miss you so much every day and I know you miss me too. I wish I could end the war and bring you home to sleep in our bed again. A year is so long to not see or touch each other. I'd kill for even the smallest hug, any day. I regret that I tried to convince you to reenlist in two years because I wanted to travel. I'm now perfectly okay with you getting out so we can live "normal" lives. I love you and I need you home … please stay safe.

19/F

COMMENTS:

>> You said a mouthful – and a mouthful that almost every military wife thinks at some point in her marriage. It's something that is very difficult to admit, but at least you can do it here, even if it's anonymously. People don't want to hear it, do they? They put military wives up on some pedestal and you're supposed to be some godlike creature that sacrifices years of her marriage without a thought of yourself. BS. Hope your man gets home soon honey, safe and sound, and hope you're able to enjoy every second of it when he does. Good luck.

>> This must be so difficult and my heart goes out to you. Thank you for your sacrifice and I pray that your hubby comes home safe and sound. Hang in there, you will make it through.

SECRET REGRET: I regret not telling you I was pregnant, because when you abused me that final time, I lost our baby. It was supposed to be your Valentine's Day surprise, but I shouldn't have waited.

COMMENTS:

>> Hang in there. You need someone loving in your life. Anyone that wants to beat you is never going to be worth your time.

>> You should never have even had to consider the possibility of abuse and its possible implications. It was not your fault. There is someone out there who will love you unconditionally and will never hurt you, and that is no more than you deserve. Stay strong.

>> (Update from the original poster) This is my post, and it's taken a while but I'm finally getting back out there. I'm learning to trust. I've learned not to accept being treated poorly again. The event happened in February, and now in August, I can say I'm glad because it finally set me free. You abandoning me let me become who I wanted to be, who I knew I was going to be, and for that I thank you. Thank you for breaking my heart, for causing me an incredible amount of pain because when I lost the baby, my fiancé, and the home I had come to love, I also lost the weight and burden that was holding me back. I lost everything in one night, and I've gained more back than I ever thought possible.

SECRET REGRET: I regret losing touch with you. I regret that we grew apart. I regret that I let something as trivial as high school cliques be the demise of our friendship. I regret that I didn't respond to the birthday letter you sent me. Maybe if I had, maybe if we'd had the chance to talk, this would've been easier. Maybe not.

I regret that you got that stupid motorcycle. I hate that it took your life.

I regret that I never got the chance to tell you how much you meant to me. I regret not telling you that you were the best friend I've ever had. I regret not telling you how amazing you are everyday that you were alive. I regret not saying, "I love you" one more time before you died.

I regret that I couldn't save you … because you saved me so many times … more than you ever knew.

But most of all, I regret that neither of us believe in God because maybe then I could believe that you're reading this now. I could believe that you hear me when I cry your name at night.

I could believe that you know that I love you, that I never stopped loving you, and that I was a better person because of you. I regret that I'll never get to say these words to you again.

I love you Justin.

I miss you more than I could ever put into words.

Female 19

COMMENTS:

>> I know that for the most part, advice sort of bounces off of you when you're grieving. But believe me when I say that NO ONE truly lives "as though they'll die tomorrow." Or as though someone they love will die tomorrow. You need to move forward and stop blaming yourself for not saying this or not doing that. Justin sounds like he was a great person, and I'm sure he wouldn't have wanted that.

SECRET REGRET: If I could change one thing – I'd have treated my wife with more respect. I wouldn't have spoken down to her and drove her to eventually leave me. I would have done a lot of the same things, but they would have been driven by heart. She is visiting on Wednesday so that we can settle financially. Although I'll not tell her how I feel, as she is so much happier without me. I can watch her blossom from a distance and if things were meant to be, I'll have her to hold once more.

Dearest Samantha, I am so sorry. xX

SECRET REGRET: I would have never went to work for a "friend." This dream job quickly turned into a nightmare. The working relationship killed our friendship, however, it opened my eyes to the kind of person this individual really was – a total raving bitch who was willing to do whatever it took to advance her career at the expense of those who worked for her!

SECRET REGRET: I regret feeling like I have to use people to advance in life.

I regret not changing my gender at an earlier age than 19.

www.SecretRegrets.com

I regret having to worry for the rest of my life if I'm going to be "found out" about my past as a male, especially since I am now starting to become recognized.

I regret loving prescription sedatives as much as I do.

I regret not being able to open up to a "friend" in real life and having to resort to anonymously posting my feelings on this website. I regret that most people don't appreciate what they have until it's too late.

COMMENTS:

>> You have an amazing amount of courage and strength for even being so certain and comfortable in who you knew you wanted to be to even go through with the operation. I applaud you for that. You can do it! Just be strong. There are people out there who will understand and accept you!

>> You're fine, hun. You're living in your true body now. People will accept and love that, and if not they are not worth it. Get help for the sedatives. Sometimes addiction is in your mind, you don't really need them. You can escape that. But you can't escape who you are. Tell who you wish, but remember, if the whole world found out – how bad would it be, really? Sometimes `rrrip` like a Band-Aid is the best solution, and it will make you feel sooooo much better. Your supporters will rally, your nay-sayers will abandon you, and you will be surrounded by the gold that is left. And about the friend thing – sometimes the internet is the best place to post anonymous feelings. Unlike prayer, you actually get feedback. Good luck!

SECRET REGRET: I am finally getting my chance to relive what I'd like to have done differently. If I had it to do all over again, I would have found him after he left without a word. But after 15 years, we have reconnected and the same feelings are there. It is almost like we just saw each other last week. I hope that this time we both get it right.

SECRET REGRET: I regret not taking college seriously. I partied the entire time and ended up pregnant my senior year. Looking back, I could have done so much more, but I chose to let the freedom overwhelm me and let a terrific education pass me by.

COMMENTS:

>> Just in time for my first day of school! Thanks!

>> I'm supposed to graduate from my jr. college in the spring, and then transfer to a 4-year school to finish up my education. So far I have been getting straight A's and B's, while still balancing a little partying here and there. Two days ago I found out I was pregnant. 19/F

>> Thank you so much for helping me to make the decision to stay away from the parties until I've gotten my education. I have been debating back and forth and what you said helped a lot. There will always be parties later in life and college is not about the parties. F/18

SECRET REGRET: I regret telling my classmates that a mentally disabled girl should go jump in the dumpster because she was a piece of garbage. I wanted people to like me, and I've regretted saying that ever since. It hurts me every day. I hope she is doing well now because it breaks my heart just thinking of that moment. That was 8 years ago.

COMMENTS:

>> I also made fun of a classmate that was mentally challenged in junior high. He confronted me about it, and he ended up nearly beating the shit out of me in front of my friends. I deserved everything I had coming to me, and I regret to this day being so mean and shallow. C.R., I'm sorry.

>> People with disabilities are people first. I am an advocate for them and take the time to educate my family and friends. I see all people as people first then the difference as secondary. We should all do the same because that person with a disability is someone's child, sis, bro and they are loved.

>> I was pretty consistently bullied from nursery school on. When I was in 7th grade, (trying, I suppose to be one of the crowd) I threw a note at a pudgy, dirty, smelly girl who avoided and was avoided by everyone. The note read, "You stink." As it rolled across the lunch table, I was appalled at what I'd done. She read it with no change of expression. I never got up the courage to apologize. Several years later, she committed suicide, and it came out that she had been kept in awful conditions and been regularly beaten and sexually abused. I'll be 62 pretty soon, and I still think of her and how I added to her misery. Before that day, I'd always been one to stick up for the underdog, and I've been trying to make up for that one evil act ever since.

www.SecretRegrets.com

SECRET REGRET: I would never have started talking to her. I hurt you very badly, and although at the time I knew I loved you – but she seemed exciting and new. Even though we got back together and are still together, I killed a part of our relationship. A part that we can never get back, no matter how hard I try. I betrayed you and your trust and that kills me inside, to know I willfully hurt the person that loved me for all of my good points as well as the bad. I treated you with disrespect, after I promised you I never would.

Thank you for staying with me and I will keep trying to regain that something that I threw away.

SECRET REGRET: I wouldn't have fallen in love with you, my best friend.

I'm sorry bro.

22/M

SECRET REGRET: If I had a chance to do one thing differently in my life, I would have realized earlier that regret is a waste of time. We all do the best we can with the information and understanding we have. Looking back and questioning one's decisions with the crystal clear vision of hindsight is a game nobody can win. So please stop. Let go. Live in the now, man. We have all done dumb stuff. We're human. Nobody is perfect, and nobody expects YOU to be.

Male, 36

COMMENTS:

>> Thank you so much for your post and reminding me to live in the now.

>> Yes, I have regrets and wish I'd done things differently. Until I read your post I was starting to relive all the horrible feelings that well up in me when I think of the past and my mistakes. I can only hope to have learned from my mistakes, and am now an older but wiser person who can feel

compassion for my younger self. And go on with my life, optimistic for the future. Again, thank you for reminding me. That it is today that counts. I have lived, loved, and learned. I think your post may have saved me from wallowing in negative feelings about something I cannot change. Instead I am going to think positive knowing that time is my only real currency in life and I am not going to waste it reliving my past failures. Thank you.

SECRET REGRET: I would have never permed my mullet – but it was the 80's!

Age 43; Male

SECRET REGRET: If I had a second chance to do ONE thing differently in my life, I would never have slept with him, because then I wouldn't have spent several years afterward checking my son's features for similarities to him. I know now that he's my husband's son, but those were some awful years, not knowing.

Age 36, Female

SECRET REGRET: I regret saying "yes" when you asked me to marry you. I didn't want to hurt your feelings. After all, you're a poor college student who spent $2000 on a ring. You say you can't imagine your life without me, well ... I can imagine mine without you. I'm sorry I didn't tell you sooner.

22/F

COMMENTS:
>> Oh Shit.

>> I could say the same thing, except my husband didn't pay for all of the ring — I paid for half! I moved out a week ago and we haven't even been married a year ... and I couldn't be happier :)

SECRET REGRET: If I could get a second chance, I would tell those girls that they aren't the only ones pretending ... I am pretending too. Pretending to be their friend. I hate those girls. I know who my real friends are, do they? Age:18

SECRET REGRET: I would have learned to say "no" and stick with it rather than let people talk me into acts that were life altering. I'd have made my children go to college and been more focused on helping them find a successful career path. And I'd have helped my dad more seeing his invention get to market. And I'd have followed through on my own ideas and inventions with more perseverance ... because I'd be rich right now. Basically, I'd not have been such an idiot, and been reaching out more to help others.

SECRET REGRET: If I had a second chance, I would go back and tell you exactly how I felt when I felt it. It's too easy for you to brush everything aside now. I wish it were easier to let you know how much you changed me. For the worse. 20/F

SECRET REGRET: I would have never given my first kiss to a stranger on the Greyhound because I can't get it back and he tasted gross.

SECRET REGRET: If I had a second chance, I would not have loved him. I would have never accepted his invitation. I would have never even looked at him. He dared me to dream, and I did, unrealistic dreams that hinged upon his presence. He never had any intention on being here. I was grounded before I met him, and I'm shattered to pieces on the ground now that he's gone. And no matter how hard I try, I have yet to be able to put the pieces together since.

SECRET REGRET: I regret that I did not file for a divorce immediately after the first time you screamed and threw things at me – in front of the kids. Because the kids then get a negative impression of married life, and will likely behave similarly in their marriages when they grow up.

It's not your fault, I understand that you yourself were brought up in a similar household. But, there is no need to pass on the same characteristics to our kids.

M/36

COMMENTS:

>> It's pretty sad that my jaw dropped when I saw that a male wrote this.

>> I'm 16, and my dad does the same thing, and I want nothing more than for my parents to divorce. They've tried therapy, talking, everything, yet nothing helps. Is it selfish that I would rather them break up than deal with his drinking and temper? I honestly don't know.

>> Divorce isn't the only option, family therapy or marital therapy are wonderful options, and can create peaceful homes!

SECRET REGRET: If I could do one thing differently, I would have given your mother the letter when she showed up unexpectedly at the door. I would have told her that it's okay, even though it's not. I would have.

F/17

SECRET REGRET: If I had a second chance to do ONE thing differently in my life, I would redo my entire high school life because there, all my fears, all the disappointments, and all the regrets had to do with those four agonizing years of hell. It showed a side of me I wish I would have never become.

F/17

COMMENTS:

>> Life is so much more than high school! I promise it gets better!

>> True story. Wait until you go to college. Life actually begins.

SECRET REGRET: I would have left my ex sooner to really find out who I was. Now I know but it would have been great to get here quicker.

SECRET REGRET: I regret still thinking about you five years later. We never even had anything more than a friendship and that one almost-kiss in high school. I regret allowing myself to think you are really a superhero, because I always felt so safe when you were around. I regret not having followed through when I should have held hands with you and skipped down the back hall. I regret leaving the last day of school having not seen you. I regret seeing you at the mall when I was nine months pregnant and feeling like I had failed you somehow. I regret still looking for you everywhere I go, even though I am sure you won't be there.

Most of all I regret dreaming about you at night. It only makes me feel like I am cheating on my husband and son.

JUST GET OUT OF MY HEAD.
Female 22

SECRET REGRET: I would have kissed you back instead of saying we are better off as friends when we were in your room late that night in the summer of 1994.

SECRET REGRET: I regret telling you I wasn't pregnant when I really was.

His name was Drake.

He is my angel.

23*f

COMMENTS:

>> Me too. He was your junior. I miss him everyday.

SECRET REGRET: I would have accepted who I am, instead of living my whole life trying to be what others think I should be.

SECRET REGRET: If I could do one thing over I would have told him I was ending it to his face. I still loved him, and I was so afraid of hurting him that I waited until I was two hundred miles away to rip his heart out over the phone.

For all his faults, he loved me and he deserved better than that. I hope someday he'll forgive me for it. F/19

SECRET REGRET: I regret that I didn't meet you before you met her. I know that the experiences you had with her make you the man you are now, but it's because of those experiences that you can't love me as fully as you loved her. As your wife, I love you completely and I know that you love me very much. But I also know that she hardened your heart, and although I'll try my hardest for the rest of our lives, I don't think that part of your heart will ever come back. F/23

COMMENTS:

>> I am the other girl. The first love, the one who got everything and threw it all away. The girl who hurt him and hardened his heart. And I am here to tell you that you are getting the best of him. He is an amazing man, a peaceful soul that has so very much to offer, and I regret hurting him. I still love him, but he loves you too much to ever reconsider my love or listen to my apologies. I'm just the mistake he had to make to get to you. He chose you. Be secure in that love. It's worth the world.

SECRET REGRET: I regret the day that I didn't tell you I was gay when you asked. It still haunts me.

COMMENTS:

>> I know this is not you, but if it were, I would say I asked because I wanted to know you better ... not because I wanted to judge you or put the squeeze on you. I would have accepted you for who you are. The answer would not have changed my opinion of you. I hope that by asking I did not hurt you. The thought that I did tears me up inside. I have tried so hard to just forget what happened, but I can't. I still think about you every day. If I could undo everything that happened I would. I am sorry and I wish you would forgive me.

SECRET REGRET: I slept with my boyfriend's best friend while we were broke up. We vowed to never tell anyone. Now 17 months, one engagement ring, and a baby later ... I still hate myself for never telling him.

SECRET REGRET: I regret that you have to leave me. I have walked through hell in my few years on this planet, and on the other side of divorce, betrayal, cancer, radiation, 50 lb weight loss, hair loss and not even feeling like a woman anymore – I found you.

You came with your own set of obstacles, but after all I had been through, it seemed like a cakewalk. I know what people around us say. Like any interracial couple, our own people look at us like traitors and we are stereotyped by everyone else. It's the hardest thing I have ever done, but I love you so, so much.

You made me laugh when I was sad. You were at every surgery, biopsy, and test, all the things that shake me to the core – you were beside me and you never had to be. When I was too sick to eat and losing too much weight you were there to convince me to take 2 more bites. I guess what I am trying to say is that I have come to depend on you.

I regret that because you got in a car accident (which can happen to anyone any day so count your blessings) when you were 18 (over a decade ago) that you are now a felon. I regret that even though I am a single mother and completely alone in this world, I could not get help with my medical bills. I never wanted any sort of public assistance, just a medical card, and I made about 40 dollars a month too much. Now I am stuck with around $300,000 in medical bills and have no credit. I regret that after 6 months of begging landlords and apartment complexes, that no one would rent to a black felon and a white girl with that much debt.

Things are not always what they seem. I regret that I am losing my true love, and the only person I have had on my side throughout all of this.

Happy 1st anniversary Big Daddy, I regret that come tomorrow you will be on a train to Illinois with my heart, and I will never see you again.

24/f

COMMENTS:

>> Don't let him go ... love is suppose to overcome any obstacle ... it's cliché but if he means so much to you and you mean so much to him (which you must if he stayed by your side through all you went through) don't let him go ... there are ways to get rid of debt, and back on your feet ... it'll be hard but you'll have each other ... Don't let him go!

>> Fight for your love like you did cancer. Good luck to you, I know you'll find a way out!

SECRET REGRET: I would have never covered for my brother's drinking problem.

SECRET REGRET: I regret wanting to be popular and well liked. I got my wish but the grass isn't greener over here. I've lost my mom's trust due to partying, my true friends due to being selfish, and my respect for myself. I have everything I've ever wanted and all I want is for it to all go away.

15/F

SECRET REGRET: I regret that I got married so young, and that I settled for someone who would rather be mothered than to treat me like I'm anything special. I've so settled into my domestic role that I forgot what passion was like, and what it meant to feel sought after. I forgot what it was like to be held tightly in a man's arms, to have doors opened for me. I was happy. I was devout to my husband and to my God. I was happy with the feeling of neutrality and my heart was right with Christ.

Then I met you and now I cannot get enough of you. I cannot listen to the Christian radio station anymore, because it reminds me that even though we didn't have sex, we did so much, and I felt so right in your arms. I can hardly look at my husband. I wish I were detached so we could keep doing this, but one mistake is bad enough, and if I see you again ... it will be an affair.

COMMENTS:

>> Whoever left this regret, thank you. I was about to get married and reading your secret made me take a step back and realize that I was about to walk into the same situation. You have my gratitude.

SECRET REGRET: I regret hoarding pills for when the pain gets too bad. I wish I weren't such a coward.

F/50

COMMENTS:

>> I used to do that too. I felt so relieved when I finally managed to throw them away. I think they were a weird "safety net," but all the time I had them I couldn't move forward. Please know that you're not alone, and you're not a coward. I for one care about your well being.

>> As the child of a woman that has done this, know that the people around you care, even when it doesn't seem like it. Don't drown yourself in those pills. Seek help, please! There are other alternatives. Those who love you see your pain and their hearts break for you, but they don't know how to help you. Reach out!

>> (Update from the original poster, 2 months later) I am the OP and I wanted you to know that I no long hoard pills. I have had some serious "come to Jesus" talks with myself and realize there is much more to my life than pain. The pills are gone and my spirit is back. Thank you all for your kind words.

SECRET REGRET: If I had a second chance to do ONE thing differently in my life, I would have fought for us, like you did, because I still love you. Now I'm married and he's raising our kids and I wish more than anything that it was you.

F/25

SECRET REGRET: Mom ... Dad ... It wasn't who you think it was. I was only 12 and completely terrified. He was 18, and had mild mental retardation. I'm still not over it or even remotely okay. I'm asking for help tomorrow. Thank you for allowing me to share my secret and largest regret. One day, he will no longer dominate my thoughts, decisions and dreams. I will be FREE.

F/16

COMMENTS:

>> I am so glad that you are asking for help. You've been through hell, now it's time to start the healing process. Good luck to you. You deserve to be happy again!

>> You will walk away healed. You're already half way there by moving forward with getting help. In my prayers ... bless you!

SECRET REGRET: I regret that I have ABSOLUTELY NO confidence in my body. You are a 24-year-old male who wants his girlfriend to prance around in a bikini and I regret that I'm a 21-year-old girl who can't do that. Swimming is one of your favorite pastimes and I regret having to go on about how much I HATE swimming, just so I don't have to say I really won't go because I am too embarrassed. I regret that ALL of your friends and their friends have swimming parties and river trips that I can't go to because I would feel like a whale around all those thinner girls. I regret that you honestly believe I would look just as good, but you only think that because I try to hide myself and we only have sex in the dark.

I regret that I'm supposed to be in the prime of my life, but I can't even wear a pair of shorts and I won't wear a skirt or dress without tights underneath. Not just for you, but for me as well. I regret that I can't just make the best of what I have. I regret with every ounce of my being that I want so much to look like those girls on lookbook or all over television and the media ... because it's physically impossible.

I regret that I think mirrors lie to me, when I do appear to look good. I wish I could be free of this body.

21/f

COMMENTS:

>> To be thin isn't to be beautiful. Being beautiful is to be happy and confident of who you are and what you are. Even myself at an average weight feels insecure around girls in general. But I'll tell you the truth, girl to girl, when I see a girl who is confident in her being – that's when I'm jealous! Thick or thin; that's when she's gorgeous.

>> He can't love you if you do not love yourself.

SECRET REGRET: If I had a second chance I would have called an ambulance for you. You're nighttime meds have made you act that way before, so instead of being cautious I was mad at you.

My God, I was mad at you because you were stumbling around and I had to take care of you again. I am so sorry.

If I had that second chance, I would have made that call that would have saved your life Dad…. that or switch places with you. …I think I'll die without you. I'm so sorry.

And the last thing I did was yell at you, so you could hear me, to get up and try and move around.

Please forgive me Daddy. Or take me with you.

COMMENTS:

>> Your father only can remember his love for you now that he has passed. Please do him justice by only wrapping yourself around the wonderful memories he has left for you.

>> I'm speaking to you as a parent. Your father does not, could not, blame you for this. He would be crushed if he knew you were blaming yourself. There is a plan for all of us, even if we don't understand it, and what happened is part of that plan. Honor your father and live your life to its fullest. That is our greatest wish and desire as parents. More than that, know that he loves you.

SECRET REGRET: I regret when you came to me the night before your wedding, crying and telling me that it should have been me. I regret telling you that you should go ahead and marry her, because she's having your baby. If I could take it back now, I would.

Because after 12 years, you're still the only person I want to be with.

COMMENTS:

>> You remind me of the girl I loved, who I can't be with, because I married the girl I got pregnant. I secretly hope she loves me still, as I know not a day has passed that I haven't missed her.

>> You will never forget him, but hopefully someday you will meet someone who you will fall in love with, and instead of being sad, you'll be happy you once had him in your life.

SECRET REGRET: I regret that I wanted to hate you and I cried hoping you weren't going to be born. I felt you were going to ruin my life, but the minute I saw you last week for the first time and looked into your gorgeous little blue eyes, I loved you from the bottom of my heart. You are perfect in every way and you have changed my life forever.

COMMENTS:

>> Well all I can say is that it's obviously turned out exactly the way it was meant to, and you deserve the little ray of sunshine which has now entered your life. Treasure him forever because you'll go through your life with him.

>> Love, pure love is an amazing emotion. Cherish it – don't abuse it and you will find it only gets stronger from here.

SECRET REGRET: I wouldn't have apologized for what I did. Because I enjoyed screwing you over and frankly, I still do.

SECRET REGRET: I regret letting you walk all over me for four years of my life. You were supposed to be my best friend, but now I realize you were barely a friend at all. You made me feel like crap about myself by showing off all your new clothes and pretending like you hated the attention guys gave you. You are gorgeous and always have been and we both know it, but you pretended like you were insecure so I would reassure you that you were indeed beautiful, without you ever boosting my confidence in return. You have no idea how much you hurt me by choosing him over me. I regret being hurt by you when you left the country numerous times to see him, but wouldn't drive 20 minutes to see me. I regret staying up all night, countless nights, trying to console you when I was on my own with my problems. I regret letting you get to me. I forgot who I was because I was always trying to compete with you. I regret letting everything become a competition, how many friends we had, or how cool our clothes were, how cute the boys we dated were or who got their license first. All of these things were competitions with you, and I regret allowing myself to fall into them. I regret not opening my eyes to see who you really are, and walking away because I lost a lot of myself in the process. I don't regret giving up on our friendship after you ditched me consistently for over a year, but I do regret allowing myself to get excited to see you time and time again, when I knew deep down you were only going to hurt me. I regret that you are in 99% of my pictures from high school, but at least I can use them as reference for what not to look for in a friend. I regret that it had to come to this. I wish I hadn't wasted my time trying to please you. I should have been trying to please myself.

I'm not going to have any more regrets when it comes to you. I'm far happier now. I'm confident in myself and I don't need you bringing me back down.

19/f

COMMENTS:

>> I recently went through a similar situation. When you've been friends with someone for such a long period of time, and then you let them go, it's hard. I still go to school with my ex friend and sometimes, I miss her. But I know I did the right thing in letting go of her as a friend. Our friendship was more damaging than beneficial. It sounds like you were in the same boat, and made the right decision for yourself. You deserve some really amazing friends and I hope you have found/will find some in the near future! :)

>> I hate that I really feel like this is about me. Every single detail describes me, and I do regret ditching her for a year straight. My mom told me she was a gem, to never let her go, but I didn't listen. Now I think about her everyday and wonder about all of the fun adventures we could still be having.

>> (Update from the Original Poster): Thank you to everyone who commented, this is my secret regret. I appreciate all your comments and support. At this time my ex-best friend and I still don't talk.

If we do it's just to be polite, but I can honestly say we will never be best friends again. For the first time in my life, I'm more then okay with that.

SECRET REGRET: Had I known you would turn out to be the biggest prick that ever walked this planet, I would have let you OD, and not saved your life, you miserable loud-mouthed self-centered egotistical piece of shit.

COMMENTS:

>> Just walk away. The planet is a big place and no one needs to die in order for someone else to live.

SECRET REGRET: I regret the fact that you were so good. A great person, with an amazing heart. Everyone loved you, and so did I. I regret I'm the one you fell in love with. I didn't deserve you.

I regret that you were the perfect man, my lover, and my soul mate. Maybe if you weren't so perfect, this tragedy would affect me less.

I regret that I am to blame, because if you never drove those 10 miles to come and apologize for something you didn't do, you never would have died that night.

I regret that I killed so much potential this world could have used.

I love and miss you, baby.
I'm sorry.

F/20

COMMENTS:

>> He lives in you ... use that spirit to do good things in this world ... I am sure it's what he'd want you to do.

>> I have shivers all over. Please know that you are a beautiful and wonderful person. He saw it in you and the world does too. You were worth it to him. Now live that life ... not the one of regret ... it's not fair to his memory. Peace.

>> You didn't kill him. The car he was in killed him. If he weren't driving to see you, he would've driven somewhere else. It still would have happened. Or, at least, that's what I tell myself everyday.

SECRET REGRET: I would have told my mom that I didn't have 12 friends to take to see the Tiffany concert for my birthday – not that she was stupid for buying the tickets.

COMMENTS:

>> Tell her now. Then tell her you love her.

SECRET REGRET: I regret what I did to a loved one years ago. Even though I have made restitution, it does not erase her lifelong emotional scars. M/52

COMMENTS:

>> I first read this post early this morning around 5 am; I wasn't exactly sure what to think about it. At first, I was angry, pissed off even, because I know first-hand what it is like to survive but always wake up with emotional scars. Throughout today I've come back to re-read it and see if I can glean any more information from this three line post. Slowly, I believe I can see/hear the remorse in his words. Perhaps it was a violent act or perhaps it was but only a verbal act, either way, it hurt both sides and I am terribly sorry that you not only carry your burdens, but you carry hers as well. I pray you find peace with yourself and your past acts. I pray for your loved one as well, to slowly find the courage to heal and rid herself of the scars. Your bravery in posting this is recognized.

>> I wish that it was my father who wrote this. 29/F

>> I know you are not my dad as he passed away 6 years ago, but I really wish that he somehow wrote this. Coincidentally he would have been 52 this year. I guess I should thank the poster for proving that someone can feel the guilt of the things they did.

SECRET REGRET: If I could change just one thing, I would have a father who wasn't an abusive alcoholic. A father who loved me, who didn't say and do hateful things to me. I think my life would be radically different if I had grown up with a positive father figure. I think that ONE change would affect every aspect of my life. Never feeling loved, having your confidence undermined, being physically abused. Who would I be today if I hadn't grown up with all of that?

COMMENTS:

>> Say to yourself, "I will survive this and be a better person because of it." Everything we endure is a resource for learning. Learn from this. Some things are out of our control, like our parents — we didn't choose them. But we can learn from them ... sometimes on what NOT to do in life. Good luck!

SECRET REGRET: I used to regret the fact that you left us. The fact that you left me alone to deal with the destruction that you had left behind. I used to regret that you didn't work harder just for me, so you could have saved my dream of having my mom and dad together. I used to regret the fact that you broke "our" family. But now I don't regret it. I understand now that I am older, that everything happens for a reason, and that even though things have changed, you both still love me dearly.

F/17

COMMENTS:

>> Nobody's family is perfect, but you can make your family perfect for you. It will work out. You will be okay.

SECRET REGRET: If I had a second chance to do ONE thing differently in my life, I would have never picked up that first drink. I have been sober for about 3 years now, but it has taken a big chunk out of my life. Now at the age of 47, I have begun going back to college and am going for a nursing degree.

COMMENTS:

>> Congrats to you on your sobriety. Please keep on the program, don't get stupid like I did and often do. I returned to college in my late 20's after failing the first three semesters when I was 18. I ended up enjoying school more as an adult than as a teen!

SECRET REGRET: I'm missing you right now. 1:15 and I'm still awake. Thinking about you. I regret I'm not in your arms. I love you. Sleep tight.

COMMENTS:

>> Me too. Every night I lay awake and wish that my husband loved me again so that I could move back into our house and sleep in our bed in his arms forever.

>> I wish this was from you, but I know it isn't. It's been years since I've heard from you and I will wait patiently for years more if I must, until I hear from you again.

>> This used to be me, but I realized we were never going to be together. I still love him but I have let go so I don't lay awake at night wishing we were together.

>> I wonder if this is B – and if so, is it me or D?

>> This regret is exactly why I was on this web page for the first time at 1:15 today! I hope you are now in those arms you were longing for. As for me, I must wait a bit longer.

SECRET REGRET: If I had a second chance I would have stood up for myself more.

When people picked on me at school I would have had a fight with them instead of backing away and avoiding them, and spending my life trying to second guess what aspect of my life they would taunt me about next. I could have been myself and maybe made more friends because of that. I would have spoken my mind instead of internally reviewing every sentence in case I said something stupid or un-cool. I would have shown off my curvy body instead of hiding my little, slightly rounded belly under huge baggy tops. I would have been proud to be myself.

www.SecretRegrets.com

SECRET REGRET: I wish that I had the discipline to be anorexic ... or stick to a diet. Or had the courage to throw up my meals. I know eating disorders are dangerous ... but I am sick of being fatter than everyone.

COMMENTS:

>> Please don't wish this upon yourself. I know to many people, it's a dream to be skinny. But it's like people say, "You always want something you can't have, and when you have it you don't want it." Trust me, from experience. You are beautiful.

>> Yeah ... anorexia is a disease, not a self-discipline, and bulimia doesn't take courage, it takes stupidity. I was anorexic for 2 years and almost died. I know what it feels like to be fatter than all of your friends ... but take care of it this way please. Search online for healthy ways to take care of yourself. Get someone to help you. Don't kill yourself this way ... you have no idea what it does to you. I have ruined part of my life, and part of myself. And you know what? I was no longer fat, but I was ugly because of the lack of nutrition. It was worse. Please just find some help.

SECRET REGRET: Mom, I regret never telling you how much you hurt me when you left us, how it broke me. But more than that, I regret never telling you that I'm ok now and I forgave you a long time ago. I love you. F/20

SECRET REGRET: If I could change one thing, I would have told on you years before. I'm tired of you beating the crap out of me because of weird text messages from my friends or a bad grade in school. I wish I would have hit you harder with that bat. You still do all those things even though I've already told. How do I escape you? You may be my father, but you are no dad of mine.

COMMENTS:

>> Get the hell away from him! You do not deserve to get hurt! Do whatever you can to leave.

SECRET REGRET: I regret marrying you. I was blinded by the romance and the unexpectedness of our relationship. And then we found out we were pregnant, I felt overwhelmed with love, but fear of what others would say about me being an unwed mother. And you were deploying to Afghanistan. So we rushed. You left. I grew up, you grew mean. Every phone call, you yelled at me, you put me down. When you got back to the states, the boys and I were at the bottom of your priority list. It's been almost two months and you still haven't seen us. I'm glad I can see things so clearly now and I don't have to waste the rest of my life and the boys' lives with tension, and yelling, and fighting. I've found someone else. He has been there for me through everything. He kept me company when all I wanted to do was fall asleep in your arms. He comforted me when you would make me cry after EVERY DAMNED PHONE CALL. He drove me to the hospital when I went into early labor with the boys, and slept on the cold hard hospital floor all night and held my shaking hands the next day until my mother could get there. He visited us often at the hospital, and drove us when we could finally come home two months later. He loves me. He loves the boys. And slowly and surely, he has gained my trust, friendship, and love. I choose him. Your stuff is waiting for you in boxes in the kitchen. Call when you want to come get them. F/20

COMMENTS:

>> Most of the regrets that I read here are written by people who have lost hope, but your story will have a happy ending because you had the strength to stand up to that source of unhappiness in your life.

>> Wow. I'm so glad that she has found someone who deserves her and her boys, and found the courage to do what she chooses. No child should have to grow up in fear, and I sometimes wonder how my life would have been different had my mom found the same courage. Congratulations!

>> That's probably one of the most kick-ass, awesome things I have ever heard.

>> Wise, smart, brave, bright and awesome. Absolutely awesome. You chose health and love. I wish you the best.

>> You are a role model to me, and I hope that when I'm 20, I am as awesome and real as you. Go rock your life and make an even bigger difference than you have now.

SECRET REGRET: I would have learned more about myself and who I am rather than about who I wanted to become. Now I am acting out that person and it's not as great as it feels. I know nothing about my real self. Nothing about me at all. I have not only been lying to others, but to myself as well. And I'm confused and scared.

COMMENTS:

>> I do this too. I try too hard to be who I think I should be or who I want to be, and I don't know anything about who I really am right now. It's a very lonely feeling to not know who you are. I hope I can change before it's too late. I hope you can too.

SECRET REGRET: I regret that when you came into my life I was still reeling from a very bad relationship. I regret that I had lost all confidence in myself and that it kept me from risking to reach out to you. I regret that I never told you how special you had become to me and how utterly crazy I was for you. I regret that I never told you that I did not want you to go after you graduated. I regret that I did not take you into my arms and did not tell you how my heart was being crushed because you were moving. I regret that I never told you how much I loved you. I regret that I assumed that it was meant to be that way and that I did not go after you. I regret that I cannot turn back the clock and re-do those most wonderful months with you. I love you Kimmers.

COMMENTS:

>> I believe your regret just made one of the most important decisions of my life for me. Thank you.
>> GO AS FAST AS YOUR FEET WILL TAKE YOU!! Do not hesitate, if it does not work out, believe me, you will never be as sorry as you would be to not have even tried. Been there, done it, and regret it to this day, 15 years later.
>> I hoped to see my own name at the end of this eerily familiar regret, but alas ... I still miss you, H ... 7 years and counting.

SECRET REGRET: I would have never divorced the love of my life if I knew that we would be remarried seven months later. I was so selfish I didn't care about anyone but myself. Now I regret those seven months and everything that lead up to the divorce.

But I can say now that my love for him is so much stronger than it ever was. And I am very thankful he gave me a second chance!

I love you honey!

SECRET REGRET: I wouldn't have cared so much what my 7th and 8th grade classmates thought.

COMMENTS:

>> Middle school is hell.

SECRET REGRET: I'm sorry I had to meet someone else who is seriously a much better match for me than you are. You are neurotic and way too anxious for me to handle. Sorry I'm not a superman who can stay strong throughout all of our fights, your anxiety and our general often-unhappiness in our relationship. But I met a girl who is as chaotic, laid-back, funny and as interesting as I am. The thing is I can't be with you. I'm not the man you want. You want a "rock" and "anchor" who will be there with you no matter what. I'm not him. I'm not that person anymore. I've grown up and realized that I'm much too much of an individual to be there for you whenever you need me. It's best if I leave you because I'll just hurt you even more later on in the future if we stay together. I'm sorry darlin'. I never knew it would turn out this way after 6 1/2 years. You'll find someone better than me. Someone who thinks and feels the way you do. Think of me as a good experience. Now you'll know what to look for in order to get what you want. I do love you, but I just can't be with you.

SECRET REGRET: I regret being so detached that I don't know how to interact with people. I regret knowing so many good people, but not being close to any of them. I regret being too ugly to have a lasting relationship. I regret never having good enough friends to have someone to lean on. I regret that the people I love would prefer to forget me than keep in contact. I regret having so many scars, because I will never feel comfortable enough with you to tell you the truth about them. I regret that no one would inquire, anyway, because they think nothing of the hoodie. I regret that I don't trust anyone, not for their own downfalls, but because I'm not strong enough to. I regret that I developed hypoglycemia and can't have an eating disorder anymore; that was the only thing that made me pretty. I regret living as long as I have; I never planned to make it this far.

Mostly, I regret existing, because I don't do any good for anyone, least of all myself.

F/20

COMMENTS:

>> I felt sick when I read this regret. The pit of my stomach went sour. I hope you get the help you obviously are crying out for. I also would suggest that you go visit the neonatal unit of your local hospital. Learn how to be a "rocker," I guarantee you, that you will see a reason to smile. A reason to have hope. Give. You shall receive.

>> The moment you ask for help is the moment the healing will start. Let that moment be now.

>> By writing this, you truly have done a world of good for me. I almost feel as though you were typing out each thing I wish I could admit and seek help for. I'm recently out of treatment for anorexia nervosa and am still in outpatient and if I've learned one thing from it: your eating disorder does not make you pretty. Your soul, morals, and hopes are what make you pretty, and let me tell you, girl, you are beautiful. When I was much younger, I never thought I'd survive after age 16. I just felt like that was when life would end for me. I could never, EVER see past it. Now however, I've made it past the time I was supposed to die, and you can do it too. I feel you are like me in so many ways. I love you. Thank you for showing me I'm not alone and there is hope.

>> This made me cry. You're not alone, there are many of us out here. It's a pity we don't seem to be able to find each other. I wish you the best of luck and all the happiness in the world.

>> Well dear, after reading all these comments people left for you and all these nice words of hope, I hope you start to see the world isn't that bad of a place. I hope you start to see that if strangers you don't even know can care for you, people around you can too. I hope you start to see that you do matter, what happens to you must matter to everyone who left a comment, they took time out of their life to write you words of hope, which means what happens to you matters to them. I hope this makes

you stronger and able to start healing. I pray that God will watch over you. I pray that you will find what you need to start truly living your life. I pray you don't give up.

SECRET REGRET: I would have told my boss just how far he could have shoved it on my last day. Instead, I took the higher road, trying not to "burn a bridge."

What a lost opportunity to let him know what an asshole he was!

SECRET REGRET: I regret that I didn't really believe you when you told me you were raped. I know I told you I believed you, but I only halfway did. I regret thinking that you just got drunk and slept with some guy, then forgot about it the next morning and needed a story to cover your ass. I regret that I called my then best friend (when I told you that you were mine) because she was closer in proximity than I was and I regret asking her to help you instead of being a man and doing it myself. I regret not calling the police. I regret not driving up there to be with you. I regret not killing the guy that turned you into what you are today. I regret being the bad friend, always, when you deserve so much better.

Male/23

COMMENTS:

>> Thank you. I can finally let go and move on from here ...

>> I've been waiting for you to say this for years. I didn't blame you, but I so wished that you had rescued me. Thank you for saying so.

>> This regret hit home. I wish it were you who were talking to me ... and I could let you know that I forgive you. It's okay. I still love you and you're still a good friend. I will move on from it, but I didn't make it up. I'm glad you know now ... Thank you.

>> This is a beautiful message, and I hope you can see how much these words touched these other people. I speak as a survivor, and others here do also. There are so few appropriate things one can say — and this exceeds expectations. Tell the person if you have not already. The person might not make

www.SecretRegrets.com

a big deal of it, but the words will change everything. Your sorrow and regret is genuine and heartfelt, and this is obvious, important, and beautiful. Cheers.

SECRET REGRET: I regret marrying you 16 years ago. I regret letting you sweet-talk me and romance me into a life of lies and broken promises. You sold yourself as Prince Charming when you were really just a frog in disguise – and you continue to believe that everything's fine with you. That the promises you make and break at the drop of a hat don't mean anything. That the 16 wasted years of my life aren't important. That you pretended to support my dreams and then turn around and throw them in my face. I regret that you're so proud that you'd rather see us go hungry, have the power cut off because you can't pay the rent than to ask your family for help ... even though they've been offering forever.

I regret that I trusted you even after all your screw-ups. Things will change, I told myself ... 16 years worth of "he'll change." The only way they'll change is if I leave you and make them change myself.

I regret having to put up a front that everything is great ... no one has any idea that I am destroyed on the inside. I regret not having good friends to lean on because you always were always so damned needy.

I regret having to sit in my car at some park typing this because I don't want anyone to see me crying.

I regret not having the courage to leave you because of your health. I regret caring what people would think of me if I left. So I continue to put my happiness on the back burner just for appearance's sake, knowing well that life's too short to waste on someone like you. I stay for our son so he can have his dad ... I don't regret having him. But I do regret having him with you.

COMMENTS:

>> I'm not telling you what to do, but I do have a comment to make when you said you stayed for your son. My parents growing up didn't get along at all, the marriage was bad, and they NEEDED to leave each other. It took them awhile but they finally did. Once they did, and they got everything well

taken care of. Both of my parents were a lot happier, in return the relationships I had with both of them became a lot better. I am very close to both of my parents who don't live together. They became better parents when they were not together, because they were happier and didn't fake it. I personally wish they had left each other years before... the change was a better thing for me. So, this could actually be better for your son than letting him watch his parents not get along and realize they don't love each other. Trust me, it was a lot better for me.

>> THE STORY OF MY LIFE! I didn't spend such a long time with my asshole, but he's insanely similar to my husband. I left. It was hard. It was emotionally painful. I struggled with money, but a year and a half later, I'm happier than I've ever been. You should do it. Leave for yourself. Leave for your son. Your son deserves to see you happy. Your husband deserves to see you happy without him.

>> I have watched my children with their dad and I the past 2 years. They put on a brave front for me, and I for them. We decided that it was time we left the source of our unhappiness and that was faking a family. Now, the kids live with me, but see their dad as much as they want. One chooses to, the other is stubborn and visits only when asked to. You deserve happiness. You deserve life. And your son, whether you can see it right now or not, is wishing the same. Sometimes, marriages simply don't work and forcing ourselves to stay together does more damage to our children than if we had made a clean break.

>> He will still have his dad. However, he is going to have a really broken mom if you do not get out. Do not teach your son that this is okay by staying.

>> I'm paddling myself in circles with you! I'm an intelligent, independent woman and know better in all things but this – still I stay.

SECRET REGRET: If I had a second chance I would have gotten myself pregnant because then he wouldn't have left.

COMMENTS:

>> Would you have seriously wanted him in your life ONLY for the sake of a baby? I would hate to know that the only reason he stayed was for the baby and not for me.

---

www.SecretRegrets.com

SECRET REGRET: I regret letting you use me ... twice. I knew you were a player and that everything you said to me was a lie but I made myself believe it. You got some of what you wanted. Congratulations. Now you won't even talk to me. I look like the fool and you can feel great about yourself. I'm going to get over this and learn from it. I'm not a whore and I'm not going to sell myself short of what I could be. However, you will continue to be an asshole. Have fun with that, jerk.

COMMENTS:

>> I could definitely have written this. The only difference is I'm so stupid that I'd probably fall for him all over again if he came up to me. That boy is so full of fake charm and manipulation. I feel sorry for him. He will never be happy if he keeps playing people and lying to get his way. I regret that I let him have so much power over me for a year, and that I was so naive and believed everything he told me.

>> I married him two times. I PROMISE you that you will learn from this and will leave him in the dust.

>> I felt like I wrote this when I read it. It said everything I was feeling. The guy that did this to me, was also doing it to 4 other girls at the same time ... isn't he wonderful.

SECRET REGRET: I would have enlisted with my best friend ... I could have been with him as he took his last breath in a world far from home. Maybe, just maybe, I could have sacrificed myself for him instead of him sacrificing himself for me ... RIP Lance Corporal ... "Greater love hath no man than to lay down his life for his friends."

COMMENTS:

>> You can live the life your friend never had the chance to. Live for him.

SECRET REGRET: It's been a sobering afternoon. Reading everyone's regrets, feeling my own and staring out the window still wondering how I got here. No, not wondering how, I have the visual memories of that, but rather why. I'm still looking for that answer.

I'm cognizant enough to know that things are, and will, be better. But I'm impatient. I'm still waiting for the life vest as I still feel like I'm drowning. I fear that although the guilt continues to haunt me and I still wrestle with the emotional effects, that it will all one day catch up to me and I will always be left with heartache and the punishment of my mistakes.

I see myself in the last few recent attempts at a relationship and wonder if I will ever transfer the rational, realistic, smart behavior that I say and think into my actions. I know I contribute a majority of the nonsense to the relationships.

I know in my head I've learned from my mistakes, but I see myself making them again and again, wondering when I will finally act upon it. I can't help but to question if I will be capable of a true loving relationship.

I know part of the recovery is saying certain things aloud, telling another person. But I'm so fearful of the rejection and disgust that will result from the honesty. That's not who I truly was, it's not who I want to be, and it certainly is not how I want to treat others or want to be treated myself. Yet, I still did it and constantly wonder how I was capable of it. It scares me that there are things about my own self that I didn't know I was capable of. I didn't know such awfulness dwelled within me. I pray every day, every day, that I have learned from my mistakes in hopes for a better future.

OK, HERE IS MY REGRET:

I became a whore when my husband stopped giving me attention and eventually stopped loving me. He divorced me 3 years ago and still doesn't know what I did behind his back. But I know. F/30

COMMENTS:

>> I love the way you wrote that. And don't feel too ashamed. It's happened. There's nothing you can do to change that. Whilst others are trying to forgive you, you need to learn to forgive yourself. Life is too short. It catches up with us so quickly, and we need to make the most of every moment. Good luck with everything.

>> Always remember, you are not what you do. Often times, there are things in our lives that make "good people do bad things." The first step is to forgive yourself, and often this is the hardest to do!

>> I feel for you. I'm in my third year of marriage. My husband brought me and my children to Asia for business. Now, I feel so miserable fighting for his attention. I feel so isolated from everybody.

SECRET REGRET: I regret being embarrassed to tell my dying brother that I loved him in a hospital room full of family and close friends. Now he's gone and I want more than anything to shout it. I love my brother. I miss him. I can't wait to see him again someday. F/15

COMMENTS:

>> He definitely knows, sweetie. Don't beat yourself up about it, it won't solve anything. I'm so sorry you lost your brother.

>> I lost my brother a year ago next week. He knew, whether or not you were able to say it. 23F

>> Brothers and sisters don't have to say all that mushy stuff. Especially in front of everybody. It is simply understood. Even when you're arguing, you still know you love one another forever. Besides that, he was probably grateful you didn't say it since he might have been embarrassed in front of everyone too! That's one of the things that makes you an awesome sister. You didn't embarrass him in front of everyone.

SECRET REGRET: I would have stayed single throughout college. I let one person consume my life, and that was probably a mistake. I will never know what could have been, but I know I missed out on opportunities because of him. I thought that person was THE ONE, that life was falling into place and everything was just meant to be. Funny how people can change, and even funnier, how you don't notice until it's too late. No matter how much time you've invested into something, there is always that moment when ENOUGH is enough. You've got to find that strength inside. By the time I did, I realized it was two years later. I should have moved on when I had that first little thought about it.

SECRET REGRET: I regret having an affair. It was years ago, you found out about it and you've forgiven me for it and our marriage is stronger than most I know. Nevertheless I spend a portion of every day feeling guilty, wondering how you can really forgive me for such a huge betrayal. You understand me, you understand the situation and you love me more than I deserve. I regret that I'll spend the rest of my life making MYSELF feel guilty and unworthy because of it. And because of the nature of the situation, I'm scared to bring it up and try to talk to you about it because that feels like betraying you yet again. I regret that this is going to eat me alive for the rest of my life.

COMMENTS:

>> I could have written the same thing although my affair was emotional and a short time ago. My husband has also forgiven me and wants us to stay together and is working so hard to correct all the problems I felt we had, problems I should have talked to him about before starting the affair. All that he does to try to fix our relationship makes me feel guilty, talking about what happened makes me feel guilty, and being in our home with our family makes me feel guilty. I am going to a therapist and I pray it will help me find a solution.

>> Life has no recipe. There is no cure to changing the past. It's the past for a reason and he forgave you. If he can forgive you, and you are the one who truly hurt him, then you should be able to forgive yourself. Let it go hun and be thankful that you really have found love =)

>> The affair seems to have made your relationship stronger so why are you wasting time on thinking about something from the past? I understand that you must feel guilty and the affair was a horrible betrayal, but don't let it ruin your marriage when your husband isn't. Try and bring it up with him. If your marriage is really as strong as you claim it is, he'll understand your need to talk it out. The reason he's probably forgiven you is because he realizes he wasn't always there for you. The only other alternative is he cheated on you too, but judging from what you've said about him, that doesn't seem likely. Just speak it out and stop being selfish. Keeping it in is only going to end up destroying your relationship.

>> (Update from original poster): Thank you for all of your insights but ESPECIALLY to the person who commented above. You're right; he wasn't here for me at a really bad point in my life. It doesn't excuse what I did, but he does know that. However what you said ... "stop being selfish." I didn't mean to be selfish — I think I felt like in order to be a good wife I had to keep flogging myself with this daily and never forget that I was a bad wife once. I think you've given me the key to moving on.

-(Comment from previous poster): I hope everything goes okay, regardless of what you do. I'm glad your husband gave you a second chance. Make the most of it and keep your chin up.

-(Update from original poster, later that day): Thank you. I didn't know how to broach the subject with him, so I gave him this page to read. He was fairly speechless, and the gist of the conversation was that he couldn't believe I was still beating myself up over something he hadn't thought of in years. He said it was beyond time for me to let it go and if I wasn't able to do it on my own he felt like we might need to see about some therapy. I don't think we'll need to though because I think I've finally given myself permission to stop punishing myself for it. I wasn't able to believe that he had really just let it go – the look on his face yesterday proved to me that he had. The conversation we had about it afterward really proved to me that he had. If he's not still hurting over it, then there's no reason for me to still be punishing myself over it. I think the reasoning I was using was that if there was any chance that he was still being hurt by it, I HAD to still hurt myself with it too.

>> There you go then. Your fears have been put to rest. I hope all goes well.

SECRET REGRET: I regret that I never talked to you about your cutting. I knew everything you said was just a cover up. I regret that because I didn't speak to you, our whole family is changed and will probably never be the same. I regret that ever since that day when we all found out, I've had to grow up and act as the adult. I regret that I feel like I can't save you.

F/18

COMMENTS:

>> Everyone pretended to believe my lies, even though it was obvious that my carefully placed and regularly spaced cuts on my forearms couldn't possibly be cat scratches. Nobody wanted to face the possibility of having to be the one to help me if they admitted they knew the truth. I can never forgive them for that, and I've removed those people from my life.

SECRET REGRET: I regret not calling you back after you hung up that day. I didn't know that your life would end that night. I wish that you weren't in that car. I miss you everyday. "I hate you" were the last words I ever heard from you, they still haunt me. I love you.

f/19

COMMENTS:

>> The day you posted this, it had been five years since my best friend and love my life was killed in a head-on collision. I lived for three years thinking it was my fault, "If I hadn't asked him to come over, he wouldn't have come, and would have gotten more sleep and would not have fallen asleep, or would have been paying more attention and slowed down and not hydroplaned." We don't know what happened, but I do know now, five years later, it wasn't my fault, no matter what my head tells me. Your friend knows you love him/her, even if you don't love yourself right now. Forgiving yourself is the first step to healing.

>> Your friend still loves you. He was just mad at that moment. The words "I hate you" should not haunt you. What your friend was really saying to you is, "I love you, but I am mad at you right now." Your friend has forgiven you, and now it is your turn.

SECRET REGRET: I would do nothing differently. Changing one moment would affect every other memory. I'm happy when I look back because, despite the lows or the embarrassing moments, I have experienced life. No matter what I will face in the years beyond college, I am armed with the knowledge and the life skills that will get me through almost anything. I don't need a second chance. Not knowing what will be is what makes life so darn fun.

SECRET REGRET: If I had a second chance to do ONE thing differently in my life, I would most definitely be more concerned about my own welfare and less concerned about everyone else's. I had no idea that my 50-something-year-old husband would visit a divorce lawyer in secret, with a secret credit card after 25 years of marriage. I was a total optimist and had no concrete plans for his disrespectful actions toward me and our children, one of whom is still a teen. I'm glad he's gone now, but what an unpleasant mess that could have been somewhat mitigated if I had actually been less optimistic and more prone to making sure I had my own secrets – like a nice personal bank account instead of the optimism of a joint account. I've leveled the playing field now by keeping secrets and being far less blatantly honest and open.

COMMENTS:

>> You go, girl! And never, ever let that sort of thing happen again. You've not allowed him to change you. You've just gotten a lot smarter. Stay strong and stay smart.

>> All too familiar story. Been there, done that. But, have no regrets ... my daughters gave me a little saying that put it in perspective ... "funny how you married the wrong person but had the right kids." I hope this is true for you. And after a few years, I wanted to thank him for all the crappy things he did to me ... and for divorcing me ... it gave me a found freedom ... finally! (It did take a while). Just remember, what comes around, goes around.

SECRET REGRET: I regret that I don't know any of you, and I keep feeling tears prickle when I read your confessions. I want to help, but I know that I probably wouldn't be able to. I've never been so affected by the words of a stranger. With all my heart, I regret your pain. I regret that I don't have the chance to love you, because no one needs it more than you and I.

COMMENTS:

>> Great hearts simply think alike. M/19

>> This is so beautiful and so true. I love you all. You're never alone.

>> Hugs to everyone that has a regret.

>> You give me hope. Thank you.

>> Maybe you can't help the people you read about here but make sure you look around you. There are lots of people right in front of us that could use a friend or just a kind word.

>> This makes me think of something I heard once. It goes something like this: "Someone somewhere dreams of your smile ... and while dreaming of you thinks that life is worthwhile ... so whenever you're lonely remember it's true ... someone somewhere is thinking of you."

Conclusion

When reading the posts in this book or on the www.SecretRegrets.com website, it's easy to get caught up in the world full of hurt that exists in the lives of others – and perhaps in our own hearts as well. A world where it's so easy to beat ourselves up over decisions we've made or avoided … actions we've taken or not taken … or words we've said or left unsaid. A world where we would give anything to have a second chance to right our wrongs, undo our damage, or speak our truth.

But there's something more that exists beyond all the hurt, despair and devastation found in the hearts of these anonymous strangers who bravely posted their secret regrets. This project has actually helped uncover a world full of hope. Hope that is evident in all the supportive comments and feedback given throughout the Secret Regrets book and online portal. Hope in knowing that whatever you are facing in your life … you are not alone.

If you are haunted by the biggest regret of your life, why not make today the day you look back and truly acknowledge it like so many others have done in this book. Fix the mistakes that are fixable, learn from the mistakes that aren't, and commit to making a difference for yourself – and for your future. Give yourself permission to let go of your past regrets – the regrets that are robbing you from the joys of living in the "now."

As one of the anonymous commenters stated in the book, don't let the regrets of your past **"…ruin the happiness that's right in front of you."** We all need to look deep inside ourselves and search for the strength needed to move forward. And if we cannot find it within, we need to rely on the strength and support of others to help us through. Turn to a trusted friend … a close family member … a trained professional … a higher power … or even complete strangers who can connect with you through something as unlikely as an anonymous website confessional for secret regrets.

Stop living in the past. Start living in the moment. Prepare the way for an amazing future. And do your best to cherish everything and everyone around you.

This is your second chance.

Peace,

Kevin

About The Secret Regrets Project Creator

Kevin Hansen is the founder of the www.SecretRegrets.com blog project. The blog was started in 2007, and to date has had nearly a half million visitors, resulting in more than 10,000 blog posts. Hansen is a marketing executive, loves blogging, and enjoys spending time with his wife and family.

www.SecretRegrets.com

Follow @SecretRegrets at www.Twitter.com/SecretRegrets

Become a Secret Regrets Facebook Fan at http://tinyurl.com/SecretRegretsFB

www.SecretRegrets.com

What is the BIGGEST regret of your life?

You've just read the biggest regrets of other people's lives. Now it's your turn. What ONE thing would you change if you had a second chance? Anonymously post your SECRET REGRET at **www.SecretRegrets.com.** Be totally honest, and be as detailed as possible. Then check the site regularly to see if yours is selected as the "SECRET REGRET OF THE DAY." Yours just might make it into the next Secret Regrets book.

www.SecretRegrets.com

If you like Secret Regrets, check out and contribute to our other projects:

www.LifeIsFunnyBlog.blogspot.com

www.MyDefiningMomentIs.blogspot.com

www.TheOnlyThingToFearIs.blogspot.com

www.TheWordsILiveBy.blogspot.com

www.MyPersonalCrossroads.blogspot.com

What's Next?

SECRET REGRETS
VOLUME 2

Watch for details on the second Secret Regrets book at www.SecretRegrets.com!